THROUGH THE
INDIAN
MUTINY

Inside the dispensary building the evidence of the massacre was everywhere. There were pieces of mattress lying here and there soaked in blood and the walls in many places was smeared with it. In some places there were marks as if bloody hands had been wiped on the walls. I saw fragments of women's clothes lying about, a pair of stays in one place, a lady's hat and one or two children's shoes ... The marks on the ground were still visible where they had dragged the bodies to the well. It is impossible to describe the bitterness of feeling and the craving for revenge that possessed us while we surveyed all these horrors. We never said a word to each other, or made a remark as we passed through, but our teeth were clenched and we inwardly swore that we would have vengeance on the demons who did this deed.

THROUGH THE INDIAN MUTINY

The Memoirs of James Fairweather,
4th Punjab Native Infantry 1857–58

WILLIAM WRIGHT

SPELLMOUNT

First published 2011 by Spellmount, an imprint of
The History Press
The Mill, Brimscombe Port
Stroud, Gloucestershire, GL5 2QG
www.thehistorypress.co.uk

© William Wright, 2011

The right of William Wright to be identified as the Author
of this work has been asserted in accordance with the
Copyrights, Designs and Patents Act 1988.

All rights reserved. No part of this book may be reprinted
or reproduced or utilised in any form or by any electronic,
mechanical or other means, now known or hereafter invented,
including photocopying and recording, or in any information
storage or retrieval system, without the permission in writing
from the Publishers.

British Library Cataloguing in Publication Data.
A catalogue record for this book is available from the British Library.

ISBN 978 0 7524 6161 8

Typesetting and origination by The History Press
Printed in the EU for The History Press.

To the Memory of Lieut.-General Sir Alfred Wilde, KCB, CSI
and my other departed comrades of the 4th P.I.
James Fairweather

William Wright has written many articles for *Soldiers of the Queen* and *Savage and Soldier*. He is a former chairman of the Victorian Military Society and the author of *A Tidy Little War: The British Invasion of Egypt 1882*. He spends much of his spare time visiting colonial battlefields, particularly in Africa and New Zealand. He lives in Budapest.

Contents

Introduction   9

1. Arrival in India – Joining the Punjab Irregular Force
   – the Bozdar Expedition   55

2. Outbreak of the Mutiny – 55 N.I. Disbanded
   –Yusafzai Expedition   89

3. March to Delhi – Storming of the City   99

4. March to Agra – Cawnpore   123

5. Storming of Lucknow – Sikanderbagh
   – Relief of the Garrison   137

6. Battle at Cawnpore – Fathegarh
   – Final Battle at Lucknow   157

7. With Walpole's Column
   – Battle of Ruiya – End of the Mutiny   183

Postscript   199

Bibliography   205

Index   209

Introduction

There are hundreds of millions of people alive today who have lived part of their existence during the same span as the last participant in the Indian Uprising of 1857, commonly known as 'the Mutiny'. He was not a willing participant but whether he liked it or not he certainly was there and earned a kind of immortality; Stanley Delhi-Force Tytler was the son born to Harriet Tytler, the only woman present at the Siege of Delhi and her husband, Captain Robert Tytler. That baby Stanley survived was something of a miracle. His birth certainly inspired several of the begrimed and worn out men on the Ridge to believe that they might win, might bring order again into their lives from chaos or yet raise families of their own.

Stanley went on to become a surveyor and died at the ripe age of 91 in Vancouver in 1948.[1] I mention him only because it is easy to dismiss the Mutiny as something in the far Victorian past. Certainly it was an age when men died for honour, glory, the old school and their country's flag, all symbols which it is easy today to scoff at. But the Mutiny, as Stanley's life and death makes us aware, happened on the edge of our memory, too long ago to be called modern history and yet full of significance for some grandparents, and certainly our great-grandparents' generation.

I began collecting books on the Raj and the Mutiny when still a schoolboy in the 1960s. Changes in domestic circumstances said goodbye to a lot of them and a rather fine library; but book collectors never lose the bug and so, after a time, I began re-assembling.

It was one afternoon, playing around on the internet, that I stumbled over what sounded like a super discovery. A dealer in New Zealand was offering a Xerox copy of a journal made by a Surgeon-General J. Fairweather. Not quite sure what might turn up, I decided to buy the item and see. The dealer had said another Xerox existed at the University of Cambridge Centre for South Asian Studies. What arrived in the post, when I excitedly opened the parcel, was not a Xerox (which I took to mean a photocopy) at all but an original typed manuscript clearly done on an old typewriter that looked pre-1940s to me. The author's name was on the front and it was titled, 'Through The Mutiny With The 4th Punjab Infantry, Punjab Irregular Force'.

I read the journal and found it fascinating; clearly its author had intended it either for publication or as a way of setting down, perhaps for family and close friends, his memories of India from his arrival in 1856 as an assistant-surgeon in the forces of the Honourable East India Company to his departure from the 4th P.I. in 1859. I set out to do a little research on the document. At Cambridge the famous Centre for South Asian Studies told me they had a Xerox of this memoir taken from a copy held by the National Army Museum in Chelsea. I found out that Christopher Hibbert had used and quoted from the Fairweather memoirs a few times in his narrative history of the 1857 Uprising published in 1978. So had Saul David in his much more recent 2002 account (though he seems perhaps to have been quoting from Hibbert). Yet Richard Collier, who wrote a superbly evocative history in 1963, *The Sound Of Fury*, based on every published and unpublished memoir he could find at the time, seemed not to know of Surgeon Fairweather's account.

The National Army Museum have a policy of refusing to put anyone in touch with persons who have given or loaned them documents, for reasons of privacy. They did tell me, however, that the journal came to them, along with some First World War letters and Second World War material, from a Mr I.H. Fairweather of New Zealand. The gift was made on 20 July 1976. The memoirs were those of his grandfather. But I was delighted to see that the typescript owned by the National Army Museum was clearly much younger than mine; it ran now to barely seventy pages, mine to over one hundred and fifty and mine also had some corrections here and there by hand. At one point near the end of his memoirs James Fairweather refers to King Edward VII and thus places the writing (if not the typing) to before 1911. I later found out Fairweather died in 1917 so he seems to have written the book when in his late seventies. It is partly based, one suspects, on letters and (since he quotes from it during the Relief of Lucknow), a diary of events.

Things to my mind now fall more into place. Mr Fairweather, the donor, gave his family's military papers to the National Army Museum in 1976. For Surgeon-General Fairweather to be his grandfather (and some of the 1930s letters from the Himalayas seemed to be from his brother or cousin), I must assume he was born not later than 1920. That the document now in my possession surfaced in New Zealand in 2007 implies that someone down under died or disposed of a few remaining papers. I have been unable to trace his descendants, if indeed there are any direct ones. Should any read this I hope they will approve.

James Fairweather was born on 19 October 1828, the son of a country gentleman, also James, from Balyordie, Forfarshire, Scotland. He was educated at Edinburgh University where he graduated M.D. in 1851 and taking the L.R.C.S.Edin. in the same year. He entered the Indian Medical Service as an assistant-surgeon on 4 August 1855. His memoirs tell us all we need to know of the next three years during which he fought in an early North-West Frontier expedition against the Bozdars, another one against the Yusafzais and in the

Assistant-Surgeon Hill of Hodson's Horse, an irregular cavalry regiment; his informal attire shows how Fairweather probably dressed.

Mutiny at the Siege of Delhi; the actions of Bulandshahr, Aligarh and Agra; the relief of Lucknow; the defeat of the Gwalior Contingent at Cawnpore; the action at Shamshabad; the siege and capture of Lucknow; the action at Aliganj and the capture of Bareilly. He later received the Mutiny medal with three clasps.

Most of Fairweather's service upto 1859 had been with the 4th Punjab Infantry, but that year he transferred to become assistant-surgeon of the 4th Punjab Cavalry. His years of campaigning were not quite over; in 1861 he took to the field again for another campaign against the Black Mountain people on the Yusafzai frontier. The expedition was commanded by none other than Alfred Wilde, Fairweather's dear old former comrade of the 4th P.I. and John McQueen, another friend, wrote that no officer was more esteemed by all ranks, not only for gallant devotion to officers and men in the field, but for his many kindnesses and attention to the sick and wounded under his care.

Later still, James Fairweather – a surgeon-major from 1 July 1873 – served as Sanitary Commissioner of the Punjab. 'During his incumbency,' noted the *Pioneer* newspaper in an obituary, 'the Province was visited with several attacks of cholera and fever, those epidemics affecting a population of 19 million souls, the duty of advising the Government rested entirely on him, he performed his task with the highest success, and to the entire satisfaction of the Government.'[2] Fairweather was made a brigade surgeon on the institution of that rank in 1879 and retired as a surgeon-general in 1886. During the 1880s he was for a time civil surgeon at the cantonment of Lahore. After leaving India in the late 1880s the middle-aged doctor retired to Jersey with his wife and family (details are missing from his obituaries but he clearly had at least one son). He died at Forest Hill, Beaumont, Jersey, on 29 April 1917 aged 89.

So much for Fairweather's career. What of the real person, his everyday experiences? A perusal of his memoirs reveals a man who writes in a solid, matter-of-fact manner. They are shot through with honesty, even to the point of describing atrocities committed by his fellow countrymen, yet it is clear that he hated to see so much suffering and death. Whether stumbling through flooded rivers or sleeping on the cold ground, Fairweather makes us understand better, I think, than any other account by a doctor in the Mutiny, what it must have felt like to be on campaign in 1857. His account is also the only full one we have of anyone who served throughout the campaign with the Punjab irregular infantry.

The published writings by medical men form some of the most interesting accounts of the Mutiny. There are three good ones by regimental surgeons serving with forces of the Crown; two are auto-biographies dealing in part with the event and the third is a diary 1857–58. Anthony Dickson Home was with the 90th Foot; three years earlier he had been a doctor with the 13th Light Dragoons in the Crimean War and spent time in the hospital at Scutari but in India he and his new regiment marched with Havelock's column to Lucknow where they were confined until Campbell's forces broke through. In his book, *Service Memories,* Dr Home, who won the Victoria Cross at Lucknow, devotes about 100 pages to detailing these events. They cross over with Fairweather only so far as the Relief is concerned. Becoming an assistant-surgeon in 1855, Henry Kelsall's dates mirror Fairweather's, but he served with the 20th Foot and did not arrive in Calcutta until 19 November 1857, the date Campbell's forces, along with the 4th P.I., reached the Alambagh. Subsequently the 90th marched with Brigadier-General Franks' column, meeting up with Campbell's army at Cawnpore for the final assault on Lucknow. Though good on some medical points, Surgeon Kelsall's diary is pithy, as such writings usually are, and gives the reader little sense of what the campaign must have felt like to a participant. The best of the three is *Records Of Service And Campaigning In Many Lands* by William Munro, regimental surgeon of the 93rd Highlanders. Serving as they did so closely with the 4th Punjab Infantry it is hardly surprising that Munro's memoirs – they also cover his extensive service in the 8th Xhosa War in South Africa as well as the Crimea – mirror and occasionally flesh out Fairweather's narrative.

General Sir Colin Campbell on the white horse urging on the 4th PI in the attack on the Sikanderbagh. The tall officer is Brigadier Adrian Hope.

The above-mentioned trio served with British line regiments. James Fairweather, however, served with soldiers of 'John Company' as the Honourable East India Company's troops, be they officers or sepoys, were all called. We have two other useful accounts (a third if I include a recent biography of Dr Brydon, almost the sole survivor of the Kabul garrison in 1842, but wounded early in the Siege of Lucknow with a shot through the groin and thus out of action); one an autobiography and the other a memoir. Joseph Fayrer was somewhat senior to Fairweather having arrived in India in 1850. His recollections run to over 500 pages and form one of those books that are, depending on one's point of view, fascinating reading or tedious Raj literature; he served first on the North-East Frontier, then saw action in the Second Anglo-Burmese War 1852–54 and here he so impressed the Governor-General, Lord Dalhousie, that Fayrer was singled out for the plum posting of residency doctor at Lucknow. About 115 pages of his memoirs deal with the excitement of the famous siege (the remainder of his book is dull indeed) and his house in the residency grounds, battered to a shell, still bears his name. These recollections are thus interesting in that they tell us what the suffering was like within the besieged residency and during Campbell's relief operations but otherwise bear little on those of James Fairweather. Another H.E.I.C doctor, James Wise, was with the artillery at Meerut in May, 1857, and later published a lengthy memoir of his experiences; these include the Siege of Delhi, the march on Cawnpore with Greathed's column and Campbell's first Relief of Lucknow. Yet, readable as Wise's book is as a contemporary narrative, it tells us surprisingly little about what it felt like to be a doctor and deal with the sick and dying, to tend wounds under fire, or sleep in the rough. In fact I get the feeling that Wise may have been on the staff of the Principal Medical Officer at Lucknow, so distant does he seem to be from giving us a real taste of the action.[3]

Before tracing the adventures outlined by Fairweather and examining some of them in more detail it is first necessary to say a few words about what it was like to be an army doctor, or regimental surgeon, in 1850s India. These men were not officially officers of the regiment but to all intents and purposes were part of the same unit, messing with them and being treated as equal comrades. An assistant-surgeon with less than six years service, such as Fairweather at the time of his exploits, ranked as a lieutenant and one above six years as a captain. Larger regiments, and here I am referring especially to Queen's regiments, had a surgeon and two or three assistant-surgeons.

In some respects Fairweather's task must have been a daunting one; he alone was responsible for the medical well-being of – at full strength – some 1,000 officers and men. To assist him he had 48 doolie bearers, along with a Sirdar Bearer and his 'mate' – a medical support team of fifty. The 4th P.I. had eight doolies, one per Company, and six doolie bearers to each one. For the patients a doolie was an experience to be either hated or enjoyed. William Howard Russell, the war correspondent, was kicked by an excited horse and forced to rest in a doolie which he described as a 'peram-bulating-bed, which was to me a couch for a Sybarite, but my poor bearers looked greatly exhausted'.[4] Earlier Russell had admitted that the sensation of doolie travel had little to commend it since 'I could see nothing but legs of men, horses and camels and elephants moving past in the dust,'[5] sentiments echoed by Private Frederick Potiphar, 9th Lancers, who thought them 'not altogether a pleasant affair to ride in.'[6] During the Mutiny there were 792 soldiers' deaths due to heat apoplexy and some of these were the result of stuffy doolie conditions.

Most of Fairweather's sick and wounded on campaign had to be housed in whatever temporary accommodation he or his fellow officers could find for them. Only in a few places did he have better arrangements; but all the more grave cases eventually were sent to a proper army hospital. Conditions here, as in the field, could vary greatly; in 1858 some hospitals had just 16 beds to a ward, while at Secunderabad the men were housed in a massive one of 228 beds. An 1863 Parliamentary report on the *Sanitary State of The Army In India*

lamented the appalling drainage, bad water supply and poor venti-
lation of many barracks and hospitals. Advances in care were slow
but they were taking shape; thermantidotes – cooling devices that
used a winnowing machine to pass air through the wetted screens
known as 'tatties' – were beginning to appear, a mechanical tattie
had even been invented along with an ice-making machine, both of
which were used in some hospitals. The General Depot Hospital at
Allahabad even had six female European nurses in 1858 to care for
the men and raise their spirits.

'The rooms are very large and lofty' wrote Russell visiting the
hospital at Kiddepore in 1858, 'and the men had plenty of room,
but the heat, in some places, set at defiance all efforts to prevent
close smells … There are … a number of wounded men from recent
fights at Lucknow, Cawnpore etc; several with arms and legs carried
away by roundshot … On enquiry, I found that a great proportion
of the wounds, many of them very serious and severe, were inflicted
by the sabre or native *tulwar*. There were more sword-cuts in the
two hospitals than I saw after Balaklava. The men were cheerful and
spoke highly of the attention paid to them. By each man's bedside,
or charpoy, was a native attendant, who kept the flies away with
a whisk, administered the patient's medicine and looked after his
comforts. There is something *almost* akin to pleasure in visiting well-
ordered hospitals.'[7]

James Fairweather was not so lucky as the doctors working in
the hospitals described above; for most of his campaigning had to
be done in tough conditions. He is discreet about what it was like
but we can guess; the Reverend Rotton, chaplain on the Delhi
Ridge, who is referred to by Fairweather, visited the hospital jointly
shared by the 8th and 61st Foot and recalled how 'flies, almost as
innumerable as the sand on the sea shore, alighted on your face and
head, and crawled down your back … and a thousand other evils
I cannot mention here.'[8] Due to the irregularities of the campaign
and the different marches a doctor like Fairweather had to hope that
his temporary rest-stations for the patients would suffice. Just one

additional problem, for instance, was that rebel cavalry had a knack of surprising a baggage train and doolies, even the ones that looked empty, were usually probed with a sword or lance.

On the field of battle, or back in his temporary hospital, which was sometimes no more than a crude shelter behind a wall, Fairweather and his medical colleagues also had to work as surgeons. First they attempted to stop any bleeding by applying a tourniquet. Cuts and wounds could be dressed and bandaged, burns treated with oil and cotton wool before bandaging. While doing this a bhisti (bheestie) or regimental water carrier would probably give the patient a drink. Shattered limbs, serious sword cuts and gunshot wounds might require immediate attention. To combat shock, loss of blood and dehydration the patient might first be given some water or alcohol such as brandy. Pain killing agents included opium, laudanum, (opium prepared in spirits of wine) and belladonna, this latter drug rubbed into the skin. Chloroform had been discovered in 1847 but was not in common use, though it was administered to Sir Henry Lawrence as he lay wracked with pain in the Lucknow Residency. Writing eight years before the Mutiny, surgeon John Cole thought chloroform a 'highly pernicious agent' and much preferred the effects of a good knife since pain was 'one of the most powerful, one of the most salutary *stimulants* known.'[9] Bearing out Cole's thesis, Dr Home at Lucknow witnessed a man who 'resolutely refused to be narcotised', though he preferred to use chloroform borrowed from Dr John Brown of the H.E.I.C on his patients.

Fairweather was probably acquainted with Guthrie's *Treatise On Gunshot Wounds*, published in 1828, which established the doctrine of primary amputation. Much rested on a doctor's savvy and basic skills but over the years, some local knowledge might be put to good use. Mrs Forrest, one of the Delhi refugees, was treated by a native doctor during her escape. As reported by Henry Vibart, 'After thoroughly cleansing from all the sand and dirt which had collected, and extracting certain portions of her dress which the bullet had carried into the wound in its passage, he caused boiling ghee (clarified butter) to be passed completely through it, and after this painful process had been repeated two or three times, a cloth was bound over both orifices of the wound. Next day it assumed a more healthy appearance, and finally commenced to suppurate.'[10] Techniques like these were sometimes learned and used by H.E.I.C. doctors. Cold poultices, perhaps mixed with herbs if any were to hand, were also applied to relieve pain or swelling.

Many patients seemed to survive the most appalling wounds and Fairweather gives a few examples in his narrative. In my notes you can read of the feelings of Lt-Colonel John Ewart when his arm was blown away by a round shot. But, with the lack of hygiene and basic surgical techniques, some wounds seemed to mean certain death: 'During all my service in India, I never knew or heard of a case when a patient survived the amputation of a leg,'[11] wrote Lieutenant Gordon-Alexander of the 93rd Highlanders. Such, indeed, was the case of an operation witnessed by Russell, that of a young doolie bearer whose leg was shattered by a cannon ball. 'His large eyes moved inquiringly about as the surgeons made their preparations,' he wrote, but in two or three minutes the poor boy, '… with a slow shiver, passed away quietly to the other world.'[12]

The causes of infection were not yet properly understood. Cholera, hardly surprisingly, was a major killer in 1857–58 though the men suffered greatly also from fever, diarrhoea, venereal disease and dysentery. Water for drinking or washing was heavily contaminated and not just with the usual bacteria but often as a result of dead bodies and animals. There was little chance to wash properly; during his twelve months in India, for example, Henry Kelsall records only two regimental washing parades in his diary. Many doctors used leeches, applied to the head, or to wounds, for a wide range of conditions, especially fevers. By the time of the 1857 Uprising blood-letting as a stimulant to reduce fevers was on the way out following the introduction of quinine into Anglo-Indian medicine eight or nine years earlier.

Smallpox took away many lives including William Peel of the Naval Brigade, whom Fairweather praises at Lucknow. 'King

Cholera', one of the most dreaded Indian pestilences, was usually combated with 'the Indian treatment' as it became known, (following its use in Europe in 1832) a chalk and mercury compound known as calomel, though some medical men swore by arsenic! Mercury was the prescribed treatment for venereal disease, mustard plasters might aid a sore throat and, in the last resort, there was always rum and hot water.

Much of the 1857–59 campaigns were fought during the height of the summer and it is not surprising that sunstroke and heat apoplexy killed so many men. Doctors like Fairweather treated this ailment in a variety of ways: leeches; cold applications to the head; enemas, purgatives, (a favourite was the poison antimony given in a glass of wine) rest; darkness; removal of clothing and a posture to bring blood to the head.

If all the above was not galling enough for an assistant-surgeon like Fairweather with 1,000 men to care for, there were also the unexpected and local ailments to contend with; men on campaign continued to get bitten by snakes and scorpions, fall off horses, or get kicked by them, or suffer other odd maladies. By 1858 half the officers and men in the 8th Hussars, for example, were suffering from guinea-worm infestation. This nasty parasite, often several feet long, burrowed into the legs and feet of both the horses and men.

These, then, were some of the vicissitudes and diseases, hardships and facts of life that Fairweather had to face. All lay before him when he landed at Calcutta in March, 1856. The Mutiny was just 14 months away, yet James would see two short campaigns even before then. Some soldiers would not see so much in their entire careers.

British India at this time was not ruled directly by the Crown but via the Honourable East India Company, originally a trading company with a Court of Directors and Board of Control based in London, though in 1833 it had its charter renewed in return for an annuity of £630,000 to be taken from the revenues of the country in return for a promise to cease trading. By Fairweather's time the East India Company was directly ruling about two-thirds of the subcontinent as the agent of the British government It had, moreover, long been recognized as the paramount power by the Indian princes who controlled the remaining third,' writes historian Saul David.

> ... all were advised by political representatives of the Company; many had armies that had been raised, and were still commanded, by Company officers. To police its own territories and to guard the frontiers of British India, the Company had three separate armies, one for each presidency. They contained troops raised and paid for by the Company – European and Native – and regiments of the British army stationed in India. In 1857 the total strength of the three presidency armies was 45,000 European and 232,000 Indian troops, a ratio of 1:5.[13]

Putting aside the presidencies of Bombay and Madras, there were just 24,000 European troops in Bengal (an area that included all of northern India) and 135,000 local sepoys.

Like Fayrer and other Company doctors, young James began his career at Calcutta and an examination at the nearby Dum Dum hospital. He swiftly details his initial reactions of seeing the exotic East and the journey up-country to his first posting at Mian Mir. Not long after came the transfer to join the 4th Punjab Infantry at Dera Ghazi Khan close to the frontier.

The 4th P.I. formed part, as James explains better in a Postscript, of a fairly new corps called the Punjab Irregular Force. The formation of this organization began in the aftermath of the First Anglo-Sikh War when Henry Lawrence was putting his stamp on Punjabi affairs. He chose Harry Lumsden, a genial and tough 24-year-old subaltern, to raise a small corps of 'trustworthy men who could at a moment's notice act as guides to the troops in the field.'[14] In a letter to his father on 6 February 1847, Harry explained that

> It will be the finest appointment in the country, being the right hand of the army and the left of the political. I am to have the

making of this new regiment all to myself. The arming and dressing is to be according to my own fancy. They are for general
service … I am, in addition, still to carry on the duties of an assistant in the agency at Lahore, and to have a roving commission to
make myself acquainted with the people, the roads, fords, ferries
and forts within and beyond the frontier.[15]

Within a few months Lumsden's Corps of Guides was carving out
for itself a formidable reputation. In fact it was unlike any regiment, irregular or otherwise, that the British had ever created. Its
men scorned bright colours and dressed for the first time in a dung-
stained, dust-coloured uniform called 'khakee'. Its soldiers walked
fast and rode faster, the ranks being filled with the best volunteers
– 'Afridis and Gookhas, Sikhs and Hazaras, Waziris, Pathans of every
class, and even Kaffirs, speaking all the tongues of the border –
Persian, Pushtu, etc., dialects unknown to the men of the plains.[16]

Encouraged by the success of these irregular fighters, Governor-
General Lord Dalhousie, on the close of the Second Anglo-Sikh
War 1848–49, gave instructions to Sir Henry Lawrence to raise a
force to protect the North-West Frontier and maintain the internal
security of the Punjab while its future military needs were determined. Initially ten regiments, five each of cavalry and infantry,[17]
were raised at stations along the frontier during the summer and
autumn of 1849 and collectively called the Punjab Irregular Force.
'A British Commandant and three officers were appointed to each
regiment, selected from the Bengal, Bombay and Madras armies,
several of whom had served during the First Afghan War and had
some experience of the frontier tribes. Indian officers and NCOs
were recruited from the families of local chiefs on both sides of
the border, while the rank and file consisted of a mixture of Sikhs,
Punjabi Muslims, Dogras and both cis- and trans-border Pathans
organised in mixed companies. The new force was bolstered by
the permanent addition of three Light Field Batteries, raised from
the former Sikh Durbar Horse Artillery, each equipped with six

Henry Lawrence who was besieged and killed in the residency at Lucknow.

conventional 9lb smooth-bore guns and a 24lb howitzer.'[18] Unusually, the P.I.F. was not to form part of the Bengal Army but come under the direct control of the Lahore authorities so that it might act as a rapid response unit to any internal unrest in the Punjab or along the frontier.

Under its first commander, Brigadier John Hodgson, two infantry regiments, a cavalry regiment and an artillery battery were stationed in each district, while a string of forts and smaller outposts were strung out in a line between Dera Ghazi Khan, Dera Ismail Khan, Bannu, Kurram, Kohat, Asnee and Bahadur Khel. Linking them was a military road running parallel to the frontier. Patrols were sent out to deter raids, gather intelligence and punish marauders. P.I.F. also helped the civil authorities by providing escorts, guarding treasuries and gaols and assisting local magistrates. Sometimes the P.I.F, officers combined military and civil duties; John Coke, for example, was Commandant of the 1st Punjab Infantry and Deputy Commissioner of Kohat.

Fairweather points out, quite rightly, that only at Peshawar was the border given over to Crown regiments and those of the Bengal Army. This was because Peshawar was a natural base from which to face any possible threat from Afghanistan. Between 1849 and 1855 the British had to mount no fewer than 15 expeditions against recalcitrant frontier tribes. These small armies usually combined British, Bengal and P.I.F. troops. In most cases these expeditions were the result of raids and murders committed by tribesmen within British territory. Operating in virtually unknown country, the British often could not identify a clear objective. These 'butcher and bolt' operations, as they became to be known, usually exacted punishment by seizing livestock, destroying watch-towers and villages, burning crops and stocks of food. The aim was to get a tribe either to give up the marauders to punishment by the authorities or for the tribe to pay a fine.

On the one hand, as a senior British official remarked, 'To spare these villages would be about as reasonable as to spare the commissariat supplies or arsenals of a civilized enemy.'[19] On the other, such punitive measures often seemed only to increase a Pathan's desire for revenge, in accordance with his beliefs, so that a later tribal clash became inevitable.

Quickly adapting to circumstances, dealing with things in a pragmatic way, the P.I.F. laid the ground rules for a century of British tactics on the frontier. Personal equipment was kept to a minimum, the men were sometimes allowed to march in native footwear and khaki was adopted by all the infantry regiments in January 1853, (the sole exception being Coke's regiment). The ineffectiveness of the smoothbore musket against the native jezail, referred to by Fairweather, was a worry; the 4th P.I. were one of the first two regiments to receive the Brunswick rifle, though two more regiments and the light companies of all the P.I.F had them by 1856. Hill warfare soon taught the British a number of hard facts. 'The essence of the tactical problem lay in ensuring the security of the main body of a column and protecting its long, vulnerable train of pack transport from attack from the surrounding hills,' notes Moreman. 'It was quickly discovered that the key lay in controlling the flanking ground and dominating the surrounding area by "crowning the heights" on either side of the route of march with small parties of troops who occupied all high ground or tactically important features within effective jezail range of a column (300 yards). Tribesmen were seldom prepared to attack uphill and were wary of moving in the vicinity of picquets.'[20]

By the time James Fairweather arrived at Dera Ghazi Khan the P.I.F. consisted of 5 regiments of cavalry, 6 of Punjab infantry, the Corps of Guides, 4 regiments of Sikh infantry, 3 Light Field Batteries, 2 mountain trains and a garrison battery. The corps had become an elite unit in less than ten years, although it was still largely unknown outside the Punjab. All that was to change during Fairweather's first 12 months with the force. 'Its training, experience and rough and ready organisation proved ideally suited to operations on the Indian plains,' writes Moreman, 'refuting claims that troops trained solely to mountain warfare were incapable of holding their own in conventional military operations. Indeed, it was so successful that it later formed the model on which the whole native army was reorganised during the 1860s.'[21]

Within three weeks of his arrival at Dera Ghazi Khan the new regimental doctor of the 4th P.I. was battling through some of the worst floods seen for years on the frontier. Six months later he was tested in his first campaign, a classic Kiplingesque expedition against the Bozdars. His personal account is a rare one, (though Medley of the Bengal Engineers also touches on the campaign in his Mutiny memoirs). Long-time scourge of the Yusafzai district, the Bozdars had been a thorn in the flesh of the old Sikh administration and the change to British authority saw no decrease in their raids and killings. Between the middle of 1856 and the end of the year they made 11 forays into British territory, generally in parties of 20 to 200 men, and in the month of December the 4th Punjab Cavalry had two skirmishes in the hills with them, losing one sowar killed and two more injured.

Then, in January 1857, a reconnoitring party of the 2nd Punjab Cavalry consisting of one non-commissioned officer and eight sowars was surrounded by 150 Bozdars and lost two men as they cut their way free. The Chief Commissioner of the Punjab, Sir John Lawrence, now urged that an expedition be sent to teach the tribe a lesson. Spring, when the crops were ripening was considered the best time to punish them and Brigadier Neville Chamberlain was instructed to gather a force together; he duly assembled 113 sabres of the 2nd and 3rd Punjab Cavalry, together with 2,317 officers and men of the 1st and 3rd Sikh Infantry and 1st, 2nd and 4th Punjab Infantry, along with 4 field guns and 8 mountain guns.

The best account of the 1857 Bozdar Expedition is in the earliest official history of the various North-West Frontier campaigns. It was co-authored by Billy Paget, long-time friend of Fairweather and commandant of the 5th Punjab Cavalry. I quote some relevant extracts:

Neville Bowles Chamberlain, Commandant of the Punjab Irregular Force.

Having strengthened the frontier posts considerably, and provided for the safety of Dera Ghazi Khan ... Brigadier Chamberlain marched from Taunsa on the evening of 6 March, and after proceeding across the plain for seven miles, reached the mouth of the Sangarh pass at daybreak. A few Bozdars were seen on the heights, but no attempt at opposition was made, and the shots fired were evidently only intended as signals to announce the arrival of the force.

The march was continued up the stony bed of the Sangarh stream (which was the only road) for about four miles ... and the force halted there for the day.

Towards noon a party of the enemy made a show of driving in one of the picquets, but on its being supported ... they retired ... On arriving at the point where the defile turned to the west ... the enemy were seen clustered on every ridge and pinnacle commanding the defile; the position was so strong a one, that it was evident that to carry it in front would be a very doubtful operation ... At daybreak on the following morning, the 7 March, the force continued its advance up the Sangarh ravine, and by 7 a.m. it was halted in front of the enemy's position ...

The plan of attack was as follows: – The 4th Punjab Infantry under Captain A.T. Wilde was to ascend (by its northern spur) the hill which commanded the Sangarh ravine from the west, covered by the fire of the four field guns of No. 1 Punjab Light Field Battery and the four mountain guns of No. 3 Punjab Light Field Battery. The 1st Punjab Infantry, under Major J. Coke, with the four mountain guns of No. 2 Battery, were to advance up the Drug stream in the hope of finding a practicable spur by which to ascend the heights south of the ravine, in support of the 4th Punjab Infantry, and to acquire firm possession of those heights, for this was indispensable to success.

The 3rd Sikh Infantry and the 2nd Punjab Infantry were placed in support at the junction of the two ravines whilst a portion of the 1st Sikh Infantry, under Major G. Gordon, was sent to crown the hill which closed in the Sangarh stream to its east, with instructions to move along its summit so as to keep parallel with the 4th Punjab Infantry.

The enemy on the left of his position had failed had failed to occupy the spurs to the north side of the Drug stream, and this was, of course, turned to immediate account by parties of Major Coke's men, who occupied these spurs as they advanced.

Becoming alive, however, to the object we had in view, the Bozdars lost no time in strengthening their left flank … and a hill on the southern side of the ravine was also strongly held by the enemy … The fire the Bozdars were thus able to bring to bear from three sides was more than Major Coke could hope successfully to oppose, more especially as the hills were knife-edged, with the faces next the ravine a steep wall, and the Brigadier therefore supported Major Coke with the 2nd Punjab Infantry, under Captain C.W.G. Green, and withdrew Lieutenant Mecham's four guns from Captain Wilde, sending them to Major Coke's assistance.

On the arrival of this support, the 1st and 2nd Punjab Infantry, well aided by the fire of the eighgt mountain guns (against which the enemy stood their ground most determinedly), at once attacked the enemy's position on the left of the Drug ravine … Major Coke received a severe wound in the shoulder … His native adjutant, Mir Jaffir, was wounded at his side, and received another bullet through his shield and clothes …

Whilst these events were passing on our right, Captain Wilde's regiment had gradually ascended, and carried the enemy's position on the left bank … This had been done with little loss, under cover of the artillery, and then Captain Wilde then pressed along the ridge of the hill overlooking the Sangarh stream, his advance being greatly facilitated by the correct practice of Lieutenant J.R. Sladen's field guns.

Major G. Gordon, with the 1st Sikh Infantry, had been enabled in the meanwhile to crown the heights on the east side of the Sangarh ravine without loss, as the few Bozdars who had at the outset occupied this range fell back without offering any opposition.'[22]

Soon the whole tribe were running for their lives pursued down the Sangarh ravine by the sabre waving sowars of Sam Browne's 2nd Punjab Cavalry. The Bozdars had lost 20–30 killed and 50–70 wounded. British losses were quite high also in relation to the enemy; 5 men killed and 49 officers and men wounded. The force marched on destroying crops and houses until the tribe agreed to meet and parley terms. On 16 March Chamberlain and his little army started the journey back to British territory. The general was, in truth, glad to get away and considered the Sangarh ravine had been 'as stiff a place as any troops could wish to look at, and I felt very grateful to God both for our success and at having accomplished it at so small a loss.[23]

After the Bozdar Expedition was over James Fairweather returned to the fort at Bannu. Soon he was to be off on the march to Delhi. Earlier in his narrative he mentions the fact that the officers of the P.I.F. discussed the discontent over the introduction of a new greased cartridge in the Bengal Army. He implies these talks took place in the autumn of 1856, but here I think he is wrong and he probably really means the spring of 1857. The first person to refer directly to this problem in a letter to the authorities was Captain Wright, commandant of the Rifle Instruction Depot at Dum Dum in a report submitted on 23 January 1857. Certainly by March there was talk of the cartridges to be used with the new Enfield rifle and whether they were greased with cow and pig fat, making the use of them objectionable to both Hindus and Muslims, in regiments up and down country. Luckily for the 4th P.I. the question never came into dispute since the Brunswick Rifle which they used had a powder cartridge and a separate ball covered with a snatch of cloth smeared with beeswax and coconut oil.

Fairweather does not waste words on the causes of what he terms 'the Mutiny' and there is not space in this book to allow for a full discussion. 'Disturbances', 'Uprising', 'Rebellion,' 'Revolt' and 'War of Independence' have all been terms besides 'Mutiny' that have been used to describe the 1857–59 events in parts of central and northern India. Even now, after 150 years, historians cannot agree on what to call them and debate continues to rage on whether it was primarily a military or civil outbreak, its causes, their geographical extent, and (especially among Indian academics) whether it was Hindu or Muslim inspired, or a truly national movement for freedom.

To generalise on any aspect of the Uprising – a term I prefer to Mutiny – is to enter a hornet's nest of contrary views and surprises. At the risk, thus, of upsetting some historian somewhere I must state what seem to be currently well-argued facts: the Uprising saw violence on an appreciable level only in what is today Uttar Pradesh, Madhya Pradesh and western Rajasthan, (there were no howling mobs trying to kick in the doors of the Governor-General's palace in Calcutta); it was generated by the actions of discontented sepoys of the Bengal Army (in that sense a real mutiny) and spread via their regiments to numerous cantonments, moving most quickly at places along the Ganges; civil rebellion and discontent generally was on a scale down-played by contemporary British historians but all of this followed on and was given impetus by the army insurrection; various social, religious and political factors all played their part in fermenting the brew.

The British in India never quite recovered from the shock of the Mutiny. Trust – in Indians generally and the sepoys especially – went out of the window and did not ever return in quite the same way as before 1857. The sepoys had been well trained by the British and fought amazingly effectively against their former masters. Their commanders, most of them petty rajahs and princes, spent too much time arguing among themselves to present a cohesive leadership. Muslim fanaticism played a bigger part than has usually been disclosed or accepted. The mutineers had a very mixed bag of aims and if some viewed it as a national war of independence then they were certainly in the minority. Most of the sepoys appear to have just wanted a better deal for themselves.

It seems that discontented sepoys in several regiments may have been in communication and warnings that something was about to happen took the form of shrouded messages, like chupatties (thin, unleavened bread cakes) passed in the night. When a cantonment finally erupted into wholesale killing – Meerut on the evening of 10 May 1857 – the sepoys possibly rose precipitately. The result is not, at least, in dispute; 31 Europeans including children were killed and the sepoys marched off to Delhi, 40 miles away, to ask for the help of Bahadur Shah Zafir, the elderly, infirm Mogul Emperor who was a puppet of his British masters. If the bloody shock of Meerut was not bad enough, at Delhi the British got one ten times worse for they had never realised what a rallying cry to those who hated them the Mogul Emperor might be. The Meerut mutineers were met by the 54th B.N.I. who quickly joined them and in an orgy of violence European men, women and children were hunted down and killed throughout Delhi. During this fighting the Delhi Magazine was blown sky-high by a few brave men while their comrades struggled to get out of the city alive and take refuge with whatever British and loyal native troops they could find, along the ridge overlooking the city. Here they made a stand while the mutineers, who seem to have been surprised by the ease with which the British had been ousted from within Delhi, caught their breath.

The electric telegraph wires hummed across India that day. The news sounded terrible: 'We must leave office. All the bungalows are burnt down by the sepoys from Meerut. They came in this morning. We are off: don't roll to-day. Mr C. Todd is dead I think. He went out this morning and has not returned yet. We heard that nine Europeans were killed.' Then, before the line went dead, 'Goodbye.'[24] A second telegram from Meerut told the scale of the British disaster at Delhi.

In the Punjab two of Sir John Lawrence's most able assistants, Herbert Edwardes and John Nicholson, immediately urged that 'a strong movable column of reliable troops (Europeans and irregulars) should take the field … at once, and move on the first station that stirs next, and bring the matter without further delay to the bayonet.'[25] On 13 May Brigadier-General Chamberlain rode into Peshawar and joined them (with two other general officers) for a Council of War. Subject to the approval of the Governor-General, Lord Canning, the officers decided unanimously to speedily form a Movable Column, 'composed of the elite of two European regiments (one to be taken from Peshawar, the other from Rawal Pindi), with a due proportion of European artillery, and with the Guide Corps, half cavalry and half infantry, and other Punjabi troops and Goorkhas … ready to fall upon and crush mutineers wherever they might break out.'[26] Canning gave his consent immediately. To Sir John Colvin, Lieutenant-Governor of the Punjab, he wired: 'Send word as quickly as possible to Sir John Lawrence that he is to send down such of the Punjab Regiments and European Regiments as he can safely spare. Orders will meet them on the march … Every exertion must be made to regain Delhi. Every hour is of importance.'[27]

By 17 May Lawrence had conceived or approved a host of measures aimed at getting help to Delhi and securing the Punjab. One of these was that four companies of 80 men each were to be quickly raised and added to every one of the 18 regiments of Punjab and Sikh Infantry and Military Police. It was intended that this would 'cause promotion in those corps, and will tend to ensure their fidelity, and form the nucleus of new regiments to supply the place of those who have revolted.'[28] It was a clever plan and, as we know from Fairweather's memoirs, men of his own 4th P.I. would help form what became the 20th P.I. This news reached the regiment on 24 May and on the very next day it started its march from Bannu towards Lahore, though events at Nowshera would send Fairweather off on a side-show.

The march down to Nowshera is recorded in detail in Fairweather's account; he graphically shows what for the ordinary soldier footslogging across India was all about, as the men scrambled on through mud, rain, heat and dust, along with their grumbling camels and creaking baggage train. The 4th P.I. covered the 353 miles in 23 days.

To Fairweather's disgust his regiment was now required to assist in tracking down and punishing detachments of the rebellious 55th Native Infantry, which had risen at Mardan on the very edge of British territory. John Nicholson had swiftly put 100 of the rebels to the sword and taken another 150 prisoners but the rest had escaped into the Yusafzai hills bordering the district of fanatics known as the Black Mountain. Most of the mutineers were hoping to reach Kashmir but some took refuge with wahabi fanatics in the almost inaccessible village of Narinji. They were led by the Maulvi Inayat Ali Khan, who told his followers of the heavenly delights awaiting those who killed an unbeliever. Early on the morning of 21 July the British attacked Narinji, situated at the end of a narrow ravine and surrounded on three sides by precipitous, jagged cliffs. Under the command of Major Vaughan, 5th P.I., the artillery shelled the place before infantry, including 300 men of the 4th P.I., attacked. The lower part of the village was in flames but the enemy rushed down and tried to cut up the sepoys. Whether Vaughan retired early to safeguard his precious men of the 5th P.I. (as Fairweather scoffingly suggests) can never be certain; he later claimed that the men were exhausted and also suffering from the heat (indeed 40 sepoys and camp followers were struck down by the sun and 9 later died). The enemy were reported to have lost 50 killed and the same number wounded. British losses were 5 killed and 21 wounded. The 4th P.I. did not take part in the final destruction of this hornets nest, which took place on 3 August, when Vaughan returned with a larger force and successfully blew up the place.

In his memoirs Fairweather tells us correctly that a party of 226 men and 5 Native Officers under the command of Lieutenant and Ensign McQueen had already been detached on the night of 1 July to join Nicholson's Movable Column. There it took part in the disarming of the 5th B.N.I. and two companies of the 14th B.N.I. at

Rawal Pindi, and joined in a pursuit of mutineers near Jhelum and Amritsar. Paul, McQueen and their men rejoined the rest of the corps on 20 August 1857.

One thousand strong, the 4th arrived at Delhi, as detailed by Fairweather, on 5 September. It had marched on 31 days since leaving Nowshera, an average of 18 miles a day, endured at the hottest time of the year. The British had held out on the Ridge through that long, hot summer, steadily increasing in number and keeping the rebels at bay within the city. On the day before the 4th P.I. marched proudly into camp the siege-train had arrived. It was clear to all that the big attack could not be postponed much longer. Sure enough, just nine days after their arrival, the assault began.

The 4th P.I. formed part of the 5th Brigade (a Reserve as detailed by Fairweather) and consisted also of detachments of the 60th Rifles, 61st Regiment, the Beloochee Battalion and the Jheend Auxiliaries. It was the largest brigade and numbered more than 1,300 officers and men, of whom 450 came from Fairweather's regiment. Captain Wilde led his men in an attack on the Delhi College, a long building occupied by two regiments of rebel infantry; but under the ferocity of the Punjabi assault, many of the enemy ran for their lives. James Fairweather was occupied that day and thereafter with a stream of wounded and dying men. The sights he describes must have been truly terrible; on that first day alone 66 officers and 1,104 men had fallen – this on top of the 2,070 already in hospital.

The mutineers made two more attempts to re-capture the College but without success. During this period three companies of the 4th P.I. took part in some of the street fighting and Fairweather tells how Lieutenant Homfray was killed and of his poignant funeral with just himself as a witness besides the chaplain. On a happier note, he records the bravery of John McQueen in helping to secure the palace, while on the same day the 4th P.I. took part in the successful assault on the magazine, capturing 171 artillery pieces.

Fairweather had little time to experience the sights of Delhi before his regiment was on the move again, this time as part of a large relief column of 2,790 men, of whom about one-third were Europeans, heading south to Agra and Cawnpore. The commander of this force, Lt-Colonel Edward Greathed, had boasted he would burn every village along the route of march. It seems the enthusiasm he had, together with many of his officers, to hang or shoot every likely 'rebel' they encountered (which would have meant a good many innocents) was kept in check to a degree by the civil officers riding with this army. One of them, Sir George Campbell, writing 36 years later, recalled the march as 'quite a pleasant one ... there were no cold-blooded executions of any kind' and most villages 'seemed quite friendly'.[29] The main exceptions were at Bulandshahr and Aligarh where bands of rebels put up a fight. A religious man, Major Octavius Anson, 9th Lancers, saw things differently from Campbell. Two days after reaching Aligarh he wrote, 'Fathers are shot with all their womenkind clinging to them, and begging for their lives ... there was a sowar with three women on the top of him, trying to conceal him. One woman got shot in the arm by accident; the sowar got up and ran away, twelve pistols being fired at him without effect ... he was finally, but with much difficulty, lanced. What the poor women and children in this place are to do without their men, who are being killed in every house, I cannot say.'[30]

At Agra, which the column reached early on 10 October, Fairweather gives an interesting account of the battle that took place within a few hours of its arrival. Greathed neglected to post picquets and went off, as Fairweather details, with several of his senior officers to breakfast in the Fort. 'Crowds of natives from the town were flocking round the camp,' wrote Thomas Rice Holmes, 'and among them were four jugglers, who walked up, tossing their balls into the air and catching them towards the tents. Suddenly flinging away their balls, they drew swords, and rushed in, striking out right and left. Simultaneously, two troops of cavalry emerged from the crops and a number of round-shot crashed into the camp.'[31] Fairweather is a little hard on the officers in the Fort; several, including Henry Norman, deputy adjutant-general, rushed over to help as quickly as they could. Galloping onto the camping ground, shouting out orders at the top his voice, Norman was wearing a sword belonging to Sir Colin Campbell and he used it swiftly to despatch two rebels, then shot a third. The pursuit of the mutineers he called 'a simple pursuit – our blood was up.'[32] It was discovered that the rebels had originally planned to destroy the bridge of boats over the Ganges and then had mistaken Greathed's Column encamped for the Fort garrison.

In his general orders on 12 October Greathed referred to 'the very brilliant manner in which the 4th Punjab Infantry under Lieutenant Paul drove the enemy out of the enclosure of the Cantonments.'[33] With its band playing, along with all the others, the 4th P.I. marched into Cawnpore, site of some of the worst horrors of the Rising, on 26 October. It was here that the garrison, after a heroic siege in appalling circumstances, had surrendered its arms in return for safe passage down the Ganges. Dishonourably, the mutineers, led by Nana Sahib, a rich, discontented and somewhat jaded prince, broke this promise and opened fire on the garrison as it reached the boats (only a few occupants in one boat ever made it to safety). Every man was killed. Then, a few days later, the remaining women and children, assembled in one dwelling, were hacked to death and their butchered bodies thrown down a nearby well.

The deed was foul enough. That it happened to British women and children was something akin to obscenity in the Victorian mind. Every unit heading to the final big conflict, the Relief of Lucknow, visited the scenes of carnage at Cawnpore – the riverside temple where the mutineers had hid and then shot the people assembling by the boats, the house of slaughter, full of bloody reminders of the last hours of upwards of 200 women and children and, the dreadful well filled almost to the top with their remains. Fairweather tells us his reactions and they are typical of many. Another of the same Column, Lieutenant Arthur Lang, put it clearest:

In every room of that little house, on floor and walls, are stains of blood … even now remain stray socks, slippers and bits of clothing.

… In the compound stands a tree, marked with bullet holes and sword gashes; in the latter is still long hair; amongst the grasses and bushes of the compound, between the house and the well, are still strips of clothing and locks of long hair … No one who has seen that spot can feel anything but deep hatred to the Nana and his fellow fiends and all his fellow race. No officer standing in those rooms spoke to another 'tho each knew his neighbour's feelings. I know that I could not have spoken. I felt as if my heart was stone and my brain fire, and that the spot was enough to drive one mad … Every man across the river whom I meet shall suffer for my visit to Cawnpore.[34]

The watchwords of the army now about to move towards Lucknow were couche for grim retribution – 'Remember Cawnpore, you murderers, remember Cawnpore!'[35]

One happy outcome of the few days at Cawnpore was the arrival of the 93rd Highlanders with whom the 4th P.I. were to forever have a close association. Everyone in camp saw how well the men of Argyll and Sutherland – not a few of them Irish Scots – got on with the wild men of the North-West Frontier. Fairweather adds his own impressions. Officers of the 93rd Highlanders, such as Gordon-Alexander, did the same. I quote from an independent observer, Lt Lang of the Engineers: 'As I walked home from mess last night after the pipers had finished playing, I found knots of mingled Hielanders and Sikhs and Afghans, each jabbering away in his own language, not in the least understood by one another, but great friends, one going on 'Weel, weel', and 'Hoot mon', and the other 'Hamne Matadeenko khub mara' (I killed lots of Mata Deens) and so on: a great shaven-headed Pathan would be trying on a Hieland bonnet!'[36]

Now both designated part of the 4th Brigade of Sir Colin Campbell's army marching to the relief of the Lucknow garrison, the 4th Punjab Infantry and 93rd Highlanders would live, fight and die closely together. Along the road Fairweather gives us his own impressions of the action at the village of Mariganj on 1 November, which was attacked by three separate parties – a detachment of the 53rd Foot in the centre with the 93rd on the right and a wing of the 4th P.I. under Lieutenant McQueen on the left. The regimental history explains: 'The rebels were quickly dislodged, except from one large high building which they continued to hold against the attack of the 93rd Highlanders and 4th Punjab Infantry. Both these regiments were now recalled, the 4th Punjab Infantry being detailed for baggage-guard. Lieutenant McQueen, however, sending back 150 rifles for this duty, renewed his attack on the building with the 50 men that remained. The enemy was engaged by the frontal fire of a party under Subadar Hira Singh, while Lieutenant McQueen and Jemadar Allah Din each led a storming party. The walls were scaled by means of charpoys lashed together so that they could be used as ladders. On the roof 37 mutineers were shot and bayoneted, and the building was carried with a loss of only four wounded in Lieutenant's McQueen's party.'[37]

Campbell's army was now close to Lucknow. In his memoirs Fairweather gives us little idea of the scale or opulence of this city. It was not just the capital of the rich and recently acquired province of Oudh, but the fourth largest city in India after Calcutta, Madras and Bombay. In a rapid period of expansion in the previous eighty years some 92 palaces had been constructed within its walls and the municipality had 52 districts and a population around 680,000 inhabitants. Russell, the war correspondent, could hardly comprehend Lucknow when he first saw it:

A vision of palaces, minars, domes, azure and golden, cupolas, colonnade, long facades of fair perspective in pillar and column, terraced roofs – all rising up amid a calm still ocean of the brightest verdure. Look for miles and miles away, and still the ocean spreads, and the towers of the fairy-city gleam in its midst. Spires of gold glitter in the sun. Turrets and gilded spheres shine like constellations. There is nothing mean or squalid to be seen. Paris, as it seems, and more brilliant, lying before us … Not Rome, not

Athens, not Constantinople, not any city I have ever seen, appears
to me so striking and beautiful as this.[38]

The sepoys of the 4th P.I. and their officers such as Fairweather may
not have had Russell's misty eye for such a romantic city. They were
bent on a grim task and it was clear that many would die in the
taking of this vast city. In the four days prior to the main assault the
4th P.I. were kept busy. Fairweather gives us his impressions but I
quote again from the regimental history:

> On 12th November the Regiment took part in what was designed
> to be an attack on the Fort of Jellalabad near Alam Bagh. As the
> enemy evacuated the Fort on the approach of our troops, the
> Brigade returned to camp after destroying the works. On the
> morning of the 14th November the Division moved out to attack
> the rebels. A Company of the 4th Punjab Infantry was employed
> under Subadar Gokal Singh to clear a small village, and the
> Regiment was then sent to the support of the 23rd Royal Welsh
> Fusiliers, who were hard-pressed by the enemy from over of a long
> loopholed village wall. The Regiment charged with the 23rd, and
> drove the enemy out. The Regiment was next occupied watching
> the rebels from the Dilkusha Garden; but they had scarcely been
> there an hour when the 4th Brigade was directed to assault the
> grounds of the Martiniere College, where most of the enemy's
> guns had been silenced.[39]

Named after a French adventurer who had lived there in better days,
Martiniere College was a school for British and Anglo-Indian boys
set out in parkland (50 of the pupils under their redoubtable head-
master, Mr Schilling, were fighting in an abandoned house within
the Residency grounds which they now called the 'Martiniere').
The 4th P.I. led the Brigade forward in skirmishing order with the
93rd Highlanders in support and 53rd Foot in reserve.

Although the guns of the Naval Brigade covered the advance, a heavy fire of musketry was encountered, as well as from two field guns. To dislodge the enemy the Regiment advanced, under Lieutenant Paul, covered by three Companies in skirmishing order under Lieutenants McQueen and Willoughby. These Companies doubled, under a very heavy fire, across the open to a long loopholed wall, a door of which was forced by Lieutenant's McQueen's men, while Lieutenant Willoughby and his Company escaladed the wall. The position was thus secured, a number of mutineers being killed.'[40]

Next day, 16 November, the 4th Punjab Infantry took part in the main assault into Lucknow. It was to be also one of the regiment's most glorious hours. Campbell had at his command 2,800 European and 800 Punjab Infantry, 400 engineers, 850 cavalry (of whom 400 came from the P.I.F.), six heavy naval guns (under the command of dashing Captain William Peel, third son of the late Prime Minister), four heavy Royal Artillery guns, 12 horse artillery and 15 field battery guns. Opposing this army were some 53,000 rebels of whom 21,000 were drawn from former sepoy regiments. The British had established themselves to the south of the city at the Alam Bagh Palace. Sir Colin's plan was to avoid heavy street fighting, keeping close to the south bank of the Gomti river, establishing a safe corridor through a string of riverside buildings to the defenders inside the Residency. Many of these buildings were set in large grounds or gardens and each was walled with a gatehouse. Attack meant punching a hole through each wall, crossing the compound and securing the building.

That day the fiercest resistance was met at the Sikanderbagh, a high walled enclosure of about 120 acres, originally built as a retreat by the last King of Oudh for his wife. It was flanked at the four corners by pentagonal bastions. Each bastion was ascended by a narrow winding staircase and had two or three little rooms, 'each giving, by separate doors, on to the broad walk which ran along the wall all round the inside of the enclosure, and having flat roofs, with their crenulated masonry parapets strengthened and loopholed with sand-bags. Owing, probably, to the greater thickness of the walls than those of the curtains, none of the walls of these bastions were loopholed, but the intermediate walls (or curtains), joining one bastion to another, and also the walls on the back court on the north face, were all loopholed at frequent intervals.'[41] The gateway had three towers; a square one with access to the flat roof of the gateway only and two domed ones either side of the entrance which allowed a flanking musketry fire to be played on attackers. The Sikanderbagh was garrisoned by some 2,000 sepoys, many of whom belonged to a reconstituted Nadiri Regiment. These were rebels who intended to win or die. They had made a camp within the enclosure, their cooking pots and belongings mixed up in the long grass amidst purple bougainvillea and scarlet convolvulus.

To get within range of the building the attackers had to withstand a withering fire. The gateway was externally protected by an angular traverse of earth and brickwork, with a ditch about nine feet deep and twelve feet wide with a narrow path to the gate.

Once Peel's guns had made a small breach, the Sikanderbagh assault was actually witnessed thus by Lieutenant Frederick Roberts: 'It was a magnificent sight, a sight never to be forgotten – that glorious struggle to be first to enter the deadly breach, the prize to the winner of the race being certain death! Highlanders and Sikhs, Punjabi, Mahomedans, Dogras and Pathans, all vied with each other in the generous competition. A Highlander was the first to reach the goal, and was shot dead as he jumped into the enclosure; a man of the 4th Punjab Infantry came next, and met the same fate. Then followed Lieutenant Cooper, of the 93rd, and immediately behind him his Colonel (Ewart), Captain Lumsden of the 30th Bengal Native Infantry, and a number of Sikhs and Highlanders as fast as they could scramble through the opening.'[42]

A lone but significant voice of dissent to this account (repeated in most histories), is that of Lieutenant Gordon-Alexander of the 93rd who wrote his own fascinating Mutiny memoir, called *Recollections of a Highland Subaltern,* 40 years later because 'There never was any question at the time of any of the 4th Panjabis having entered the breach with us.'[43] He even went further and claimed 'Very few of the 4th Panjabis entered by the gateway, and they were only stragglers from the main body of the regiment.'[44] In his account he has the 4th P.I. under Paul going halfway around the enclosure to the north-west bastion and somehow (even he could not work out how) scaling the wall there.

It all remains very curious since Gordon-Alexander, who clearly believed no Punjabis entered via the breach, was so involved in the fighting (being one of the first to get inside) that it is hard to see why he is so certain that his facts are right. To add fuel to this small but interesting controversy, no one else that I can find – not Roberts, Lang, Campbell, Jones-Parry, Norman, Forbes-Mitchell or Ewart, just to name a few – back up his assertions.

The simple truth is that, once the assault was launched, it was a living hell of smoke, gunfire, screams and bloody fighting. It was impossible for anyone to see more than a few yards ahead of him. Just to add to the confusion, the 93rd Highlanders were not wearing scarlet tunics that day, but brown jackets, not unlike the khaki uniforms of the 4th P.I. Gordon-Alexander allows that some Indian sappers did get to the breach early on to enlarge the hole and these were also wearing khaki. My own opinion, having read as widely as I can, is a handful of 4th P.I. sepoys did reach the breach and scramble through. The majority, as witnessed by many, charged the gate slightly ahead of the rest of the force, encouraged by the shouts of Dogra Subadar Gokal Singh. This is why, as he raced for the gate, Mukarrab Khan was able to thrust his arm in and stop its closure.

Fairweather was there but makes no mention of things as seen by Gordon-Alexander. It does seem to me quite likely that the 4th P.I. may have broken off in the melee, some entering through the breach led by McQueen (according to the regimental history), some straight at the gate and the others led by Paul or Willoughby around the other side.

Lieutenant Lang of the Engineers wrote that 'I saw Lt. Paul rush ahead waving his sword, and the 4th Punjabis yelling and shouting, as they charged behind him straight at the building.' Once inside the enclosure the fight was, as Fairweather says, for a few minutes a corner of Hell. 'I never heard, and such a sight of slaughter I never saw, 'wrote Lang, ' In the open rooms right and left of the archway Pandies were shot down and bayoneted in heaps, three or four deep.'[45] Retreating to a long building at the end of the garden the rebels hid behind the venetian shutters. Thousands of bullets were poured in. Lang wrote that day that the screams were 'horrible' as bodies burned. The rebels held out in the bastions for as long as they could. Explosives were used to kill some and it was here that Lieutenant Paul was killed. Not one mutineer was spared – the body count was 1, 840 killed. It was at some cost to Campbell's army; the 4th P.I. alone that day lost 72 killed and wounded including 3 British officers.

James Fairweather tells us in his memoirs of the next few days and the evacuation of the exhausted Lucknow garrison, its women and children. This was followed by the march back to Cawnpore where General Windham had got himself into difficulties at the hands of the wily rebel leader, Tantia Tope. To be fair to Windham he had only 1,700 men against a rebel force estimated at 14,000 disciplined soldiers from Gwalior and 11,000 irregulars. During the flight of the Gwalior Contingent, witnessed by Fairweather, he quite rightly calls the British officer in charge that day a blunderer. This was Sir William Mansfield, Campbell's cold, supercilious (and thus highly disliked) chief-of-staff whom he, on this rare occasion, let take field command. It was a mistake. Mansfield was an excellent desk soldier but, as Holmes wrote, he 'did not possess the eye of a general'[46] – which in his case was true in more than one sense since he was very short-sighted.

For three months, while Sir Colin Campbell pulled together all the troops he could for a final assault to regain Lucknow, the 4th P.I. had a relatively quiet time. Then, on the morning of 9 March the officers and sepoys found themselves back again at the Martiniere in a tough fight to take control of the building. Fairweather reports all this and the fight that night to win a walled garden close by. On the afternoon of 11 March 1858, the Brigade and its redoubtable commander, the boyish-looking Adrian Hope, set out to storm the Begum Kothi, the huge palace that had been the home of Hazrat Mahal, one of the wives of the last King of Oudh and a chief rebel. Surrounded by ditches and teak palisades, some 5,000 mutineers were holed up here and, when the attack came from the British, over 700 of them decided to sell their lives dearly. Once inside the 4th Punjab Infantry, fighting in two wings, alongside others of the Brigade, had to move slowly and stealthily as the rebels fought through a long series of small locked rooms. The fighting lasted from 4 to 6 pm and during these two hours the 4th P.I. suffered 25 killed and wounded. Afterwards, as the regimental history records it,

> Some men of the 4th Punjab Infantry, finding themselves with the 42nd Highlanders, who had covered the left of the attack, proceeded with them up a street, where such sharp opposition was met that nearly the whole force was temporarily driven back. Here a Sepoy of the Regiment named Munah Singh, remained alone helping a wounded European, until the remainder rallying, returned under Captain Mcleod of the 42nd Highlanders, to his assistance. He was afterwards awarded the Order of Merit for his bravery.[47]

The battle for Lucknow took several days and it was not until ten days after the attack on the Begum Kothi that the 4th P.I. had its serious encounter with wahabi fanatics near a mosque. Several men led by Captain Hood ran slap-bang into a street barricade and three large guns. The mutineers got the elevation all wrong but the guns still did nasty work and that day the regiment lost another 17 killed or wounded. Fairweather describes all this and the terrible injuries suffered by Hood.

With the fall of Lucknow one might have thought the 4th P.I. would have earned some rest. That was still a long way off and the regiment was quickly drafted, along with the 93rd Highlanders, into a column under the overall command of Brigadier-General Robert Walpole to deal with bands of rebels in Rohilkund. No one then, or since, had had a good word to say about the opinionated and foolish Walpole. Its not difficult to see why; when a sowar of Hodson's Horse escaped from Ruiya and told him the Fort would be evacuated in the afternoon, after Nirpat Singh had made a token resistance, 'to save his honour', the general refused to believe him and worse, told that the place was almost defenceless on its water side, a shallow lake, he again would not listen. During the attack the British artillery got off about three perfectly aimed shells at the gate before Walpole put a stop to it. An old Highlander muttered, 'The man doesna seem to ken his ain mind!'[48]

Watching the awful fight in the ditch, Lieutenant Gordon-Alexander lamented how the 42nd Highlanders lost 2 officers and 7 men killed, and 2 officers and 31 men wounded, and the 4th P.I. 47 officers and men killed and wounded, 'shot down like dogs at 20 or 30 paces distance.'[49] The death of young Lieutenant Willoughby and the heroism of Captain William Martin Cafe are covered fully by Fairweather. The Cafe VC incident did not, I think, impress the regiment's doctor as he watched more and more of his young men die; it was just another stupid loss of life and his railing against officers trying to win glory at this point in his narrative is, almost certainly, a comment on Captain Cafe and his actions.

The death of Brigadier-General Adrian Hope was the final dark cloud on a dreadful day for the British Army. This best loved of generals died with a smile on his lips and the words, 'Goodbye Archie; remember me to all friends.'[50] Forced to retire from an ill-defended fort, some of its occupants armed only with bows and arrows, their favourite general killed and, perhaps worst of all, British bodies left behind to be stripped and mutilated, Walpole was truly loathed by all those in his army. In fact his name, as Fairweather proves, would always be execrated by all who fought that terrible day. Sergeant Forbes-Mitchell later wrote, 'So heated was the feeling on the night the dead were buried, that if any non-commissioned officer had dared to take the lead, the life of General Walpole would not have been worth half an hour's purchase.'[51]

In his memoirs Surgeon Munro of the 93rd Highlanders had special praise for the sepoys of the 4th Punjab Infantry at Ruiya. Referring to the 'gallant 4th Punjabees', as he called them, Munro wrote: 'When the regiment joined the Rohilcund Field Force there were five officers, and two hundred and five men present. Of these one officer was killed and two wounded, and forty-six men killed and wounded, leaving two officers (one of these the Surgeon) and one hundred and fifty-nine men to represent a regiment which only ten months previously had marched to the siege of Delhi with twelve officers and eight hundred men.'[52] The situation was even worse, since 1,000 officers and men had set out for Delhi, but Munro's sentiments – including the reference to the 4th P.I. surgeon (Fairweather) – are correct. Depleted in strength, by now poorly officered, the 4th P.I. had fought on countless occasions and won the huge admiration of all the British camp.

The regimental history records that 'The parade strength was now reduced to 3 British officers (including Dr Fairweather, who it should be here mentioned, had been with the Regiment through-out, and had taken part in all its engagements) 5 Native Officers and 101 rifles; or a total strength of 109 of all ranks.'[53] This little force, barely ten per cent of the numbers ten months previously, had one more stiff fight on its hands at Bareilly on May 5th, when Campbell led an army of 8,000 men towards the town. In the ruined cantonments the 4th P.I. were vigorously attacked by ghazis and fell back on men of the 42nd Highlanders. Ultimately the enemy were defeated but not before the regiment had lost a further 5 killed and 13 wounded in the hand-to-hand fighting.

Not long after this the 4th P.I. had to part company with its great friends from the 93rd Highlanders. One can imagine what a sight

Brigadier Adrian Hope, who was killed at Ruiya.

the farewells must have been between the dusky men of the North-West Frontier and their Gaelic companions. Regimental associations forged in war are seldom, if ever, forgotten. Many years later two officers of the 93rd Highlanders were candidates for the Indian Staff Corps and specially applied to serve a term with, naturally enough, the 4th Punjab Infantry!

No Native Infantry regiment fighting on the British side lost so heavily or fought for so long as the brave sepoys of the 4th Punjab Infantry. It is also not difficult to sympathise with the remaining 103 of all ranks who wondered by this stage if the British saw them simply as cannon fodder. Each man suspected he would never see his beloved frontier hills again.

They did get back for a well earned leave in May and the head-quarters of the regiment stayed at Rawal Pindi recruiting into 1859. About this time Fairweather left the 4th P.I. 'His kindness and zeal had won the esteem of all ranks, and his departure was greatly regretted,'[54] noted the regimental history.

About half a century later it seems the good doctor had not forgot-ten the many men he lived with, cared for, watched die and buried in those turbulent months 1857–58. He dedicated his memoirs to them and his friend, long dead but not forgotten, the burly commandant, Alfred Wilde. I feel sure that James Fairweather would be pleased that his memoirs might at last see the light of day and do his comrades honour. It has been a pleasure for me to get them ready for publica-tion, add a few (I hope) useful notes and this introduction, which might help to flesh out Fairweather's personal testimony.

Historians will argue over aspects of the great Rising for a long time to come. During the 150th anniversary year several books appeared in print in England and almost 40 more in India. I hope by the 200th anniversary that enough dust may have settled for Indians to honour all those who died – whatever their skin colour, race, creed or side on which they fought. In the case of the men of the 4th P.I. it can be argued that they were true to their salt, kept fidelity and honour as their creed or, more practically, as mercenaries, simply wanted to settle old scores with the men of the plains whom they scorned. It hardly matters. There was good and bad on both sides, the British committed their own deeds just as horrible as Cawnpore, and nobody – then or now – ought to be too sanctimonious. The men of the 4th Punjab Infantry, their British and Native Officers, fought and died courageously. Those they opposed were united only in a desire to rid themselves of the British yoke, but they also fought most bravely and some men on both sides were, according to their lights, very great heroes.

Finally, my thanks to the staff of the National Army Museum, Chelsea, for their help in the preparation of this work and my long-suffering assistant Krisztina Elias, who collated the photographs and produced the index as expertly as she did on my last book.

William Wright, Budapest.

Notes

1 What is it about Vancouver? In addition to Mr Tytler I know that in 1936 a Mr Palmer was living there who was the last man alive to be permitted to wear the Siege of Lucknow medal; aged ten he had been an ammunition carrier during the conflict. In 2002 I was in a Vancouver shop and expressed my interest in the Mutiny. The owner invited me upstairs and beckoned to an old tin trunk; inside was the uniform and sword worn by General Windham throughout the Mutiny!

2 *Pioneer* newspaper obituary, Allahabad, 13 May 1917.

3 Books by Fayrer and Wise are listed in the bibliography. I also recommend *Cunningham: The Last Man*, privately published, Oxford 2003, on Dr Brydon. I am discounting for inclusion here an anonymously written history of the siege of Delhi which is attributed to William Wotherspoon Ireland, a doctor in the Indian Medical Service since it is written in a general as opposed to autobiographical sense.

4 Russell, vol ii, p 31.

5 Ibid, p 3

6 Heathcote, *The Indian Army*, London 1964, p 163.

7 Edwardes, *My Indian Mutiny Diary*, London 1957, p 14.

8 Rotton, *The Chaplain's Narrative of the Siege Of Delhi*, London 1858, pp 135–136.
9 Bruce, *Six Battles For India*, London 1969, pp 322–323.
10 Vibart, *The Sepoy Mutiny*, London 1898, pp 100–101.
11 Gordon-Alexander, p 280.
12 Russell, vol i, pp 300.
13 David, *The Indian Mutiny*, London 2002, p 9.
14 Lumsden & Elsmie, p 47.
15 Ibid, p 34.
16 Ibid, p 48.
17 I am using Moreman's figures here; Fairweather gives a later figure though he was correct by the time of the Mutiny.
18 Moreman, p 6.
19 Bellew, *Our Punjab Frontier*, Calcutta 1868, p 57.
20 Moreman, p 17.
21 Ibid, pp 21.
22 Paget & Mason, pp 604–610.
23 Forrest, p 323.
24 Raynor, Records, Pt I, p 3.
25 Forrest, p 330.
26 Ibid, pp 330–331.
27 Raynor, Records, Pt I, p 25.
28 Ibid, p 31.
29 Campbell, *Memoirs Of My Indian Career*, London 1893, vol i, p 257.
30 Anson, p 177–178.
31 Holmes, p 393.
32 Lee-Warner, p 179.
33 History, p 16.
34 Blomfield, p 121.
35 The British committed their own excesses; Brigadier Neill had arrived at Cawnpore and treated innocent Indians abominably, hanging them willy-nilly and making high-caste Hindus lick blood from the floor of the massacre site. Even worse, Frederic Cooper, commissioner at Amritsar, shot down 200 unarmed sepoys who surrendered to him, caused 45 more to die in a callous re-enactment of the Black Hole of Calcutta, then threw most of the bodies down a well The authorities congratulated him for his actions. Then, (with shades of the SS being told by Himmler to kill Jews 'non-sadistically'), Cooper was reprimanded for gloating in a report over the killings.

36 Blomfield, p 127.
37 History, p 17.
38 Russell, vol i, pp 253–254 and 257.
39 History, pp 18–19.
40 Ibid, p 19.
41 Gordon-Alexander, p 77.
42 Roberts, vol i, p 325.
43 Gordon-Alexander, p 87.
44 Ibid, p 97.
45 Blomfield, p 139.
46 Holmes, p 427.
47 History, p 27.
48 Gordon-Alexander, p 293.
49 Ibid, p 291.
50 Ibid, 294.
51 Forbes-Mitchell, p 246.
52 Munro, vol ii, p 286.
53 History, p 31.
54 Ibid,pp 33.

1

Arrival in India – Joining the Punjab Irregular Force – the Bozdar Expedition

In July 1855, I passed the competition exam for the Medical Service of the Honourable East India Company and sailed for Calcutta on November 10th, arriving there on March 20th, 1856. As there was no room in the General Hospital where newly appointed Assistant Surgeons were usually accommodated, I and two of my fellow passengers (Dr. Lindsay Stewart[1] and Dr. I. Kirk[2]) were given quarters in the barracks in Fort William.

They were dreary abodes, dirty and without furniture. After getting a few servants, we sent them to buy charpoys[3] with mosquito curtains for each of us, some chairs, two tables, bathroom fittings and cooking utensils with plates, cups and saucers, knives and forks, etc. All were of the roughest. We had our meals together in one of our rooms. We walked to the General Hospital every morning, which was at a considerable distance across the Maidan and on our return thoroughly enjoyed our bath consisting of several ghurras[4] of cool water poured over us as we stood in a place made for this.

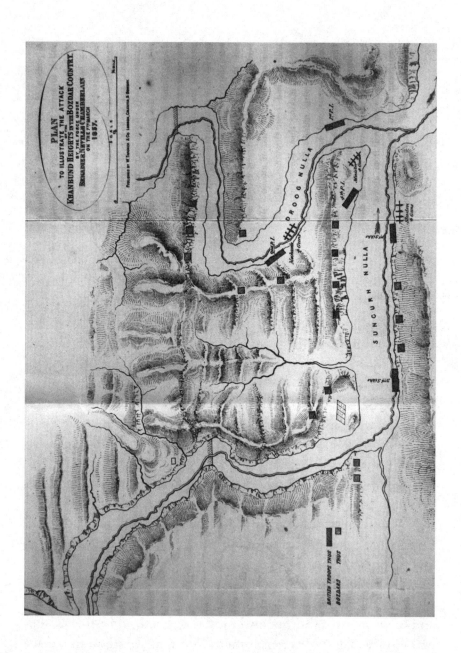

The days were long and hot and dreary but we read and studied Hindustani with our munshis[5] until the afternoon breeze from the Sunderbunds[6] began to blow and then we threw open the jhilmils[7] to enjoy the cool air. My munshi understood his work and gave me short sentences to learn, involving such questions and answers as I was likely to get at my examination, but the others laughed at his plan and stuck to their own, which was to get up the grammar thoroughly and the meanings of as long a list of words as they could remember. When the day of our exam arrived we had all to go to Dum Dum[8] in sword and uniform. There were a large number of us and when we had all gone through our ordeal we were called in to hear the result. All were astounded, including myself, when it was announced that only I and an officer of the Artillery had passed. Didn't I crow over Stewart and Kirk!

At the end of our first month we had to go and draw our first pay. This was a great occasion and we all three went in palankeens. Our pay was not large, being only for the latter part of March, but I think we were prouder of it than of any subsequent pay. In going to the pay office, I remember passing a dog just dead lying on the street, and already attracting a flock of crows, kites and vultures. On my return nothing of it remained but the bones picked bare. After sunset we used to walk on the Maidan[9] (the extensive open plain round the Fort), to watch the stream of carriages passing to and fro along the bank of the Hoogly with Europeans or natives in them 'eating the air', such as it was. We sometimes extended our walks to the band at the Eden Gardens, but the sight of the children trying to play round the band made me sad, for they all had such white anaemic faces and were clothed in such immaculate white dresses as if they had not the energy to soil them.

At first I put up in a large bungalow with Lts. Sladen[10] and O'Dell and Assistant-Surgeon Herman Bickwell, all of the 81st Regiment, but the latter was such an eccentric that we soon broke up our establishment. He was a merry fellow and a Roman Catholic and, although we spent hours in battling over our religions, it was all in good humour. The scenes he had with his servants were laughable – one day he would elevate his bheestie[11] and raise his syce[12] to the rank and so on – all apparently done in good humour and the servants enjoying the game of 'General Post' as much as he himself. He wanted to be a thorough soldier and got a man from the Regiment to put him through his drill in the central room. He then took to the French horn; this was the climax and we all bolted. I met him some years afterwards going down the Indus in a country boat. He had then apparently become a Mahommedan for he descanted to me on the beautiful simplicity of that religion; he showed me his prayer carpet which he spread on the deck of the boat and paid his devotions towards the setting sun with his boatmen. What became of him afterwards I know not.

The days soon became unpleasantly hot, especially as we had no punkas[13] and I was very glad when Kirk and I got the order to proceed to Mian Mir. We started on May 24th, and travelled by train to Ranigunge[14], which was all the length the railway had reached in those days. Here we got into a gharry[15] which had been provided for us, but before we had gone far we came to the banks of a river, where a Cavalry Regiment was being ferried over. As there was no spare boat for us our horses were taken out and we were left in the sand the greater part of the night till the Regiment was all taken over. This made it very late before we reached the dak bungalow[16] where we were to rest during the heat of the day. In this way we travelled by night and rested by day until we got to Delhi, where we halted for a day and saw it in its old tawdry splendour, before it was wiped out by the Mutiny.

As we drove out next night my eyes were attracted by the stone walls in the suburbs, only walls of mud having been seen all the way from Calcutta. Little did I think then under different circumstances I would return to Delhi in just over a year. At Pipli, just beyond Karnal, the Grand Trunk Road came to end and we had to take to doolies. In these we reached Amballa where I met my old friend and predecessor at Selkirk, Dr. Donald Sinclair Smith and Lt.

Hills,[17] my cabin companion on the voyage to India, both of the 9th Lancers, who were stationed there. We halted here a day and went on next evening. As we went along I had been admiring the ranges of the Himalayas which were visible from Ambala and after a time it appeared to me they were coming closer to us. Then they assumed a brick-dust colour and shortly we were enveloped in a dust storm, about the worst I ever saw in India. The doolie[18] bearers put the doolies down on the side of the road and cowered behind them for shelter, while we remained in total darkness and choked with dust for what seemed to me a very long time.

On entering the Punjab and going on to Lahore, what struck us was the goodness of the roads, the walled towns and the people working in the fields, in many cases with shields on their backs and tulwars by their side. The women all seemed to wear ample trousers while the men generally wore a blue cloth wrapped round them like a petticoat. The journey from Calcutta to Lahore took us just a fortnight. Now it is done in 2 days and nights! I was posted to do duty with the 81st Regiment stationed at Mian Mir, while Kirk went on to Peshawur. The Surgeon of the 81st, named Jackson, was an eccentric old man, but he had a very charming wife of whom I still have the kindest recollections.

Soon after my arrival Jackson was taken ill with an inward complaint from which he had suffered before and to my surprise he sent for me although there were many Senior Medical Officers in the station. I went and stayed with him all night as he was very ill and I was afraid he might sink under it. I advised Mrs Jackson to call in any doctor she would like but she declared he would see no one but me as he was not on good terms with the other doctors. And so I had to continue my attendance, although I knew how I should probably be blamed if he should die without my calling in another opinion, seeing that I was so comparatively young and inexperienced as they might think. However, as day dawned the old man began to get over the attack, to my great relief, and ever after I was a persona grata in the house.

Instead of walking to hospital, as had been my custom, Mrs Jackson now insisted on my using their carriage. During the few weeks I remained at Mian Mir I had an opportunity of getting a little glimpse of the pre-Mutiny days. Both Native and European troops were dressed in snowy white uniform, the former appearing to me like wooden figures and the latter, with their pale faces, like men out of hospital. The old fashion of drinking wine with each other had not yet gone out and the first night I was at Mess I was asked to take wine with so many that by the time the cloth was removed I was not at all sure of myself. The Messes of the N.I. Regiments were, as a rule, better managed than those of the British Regiments. In Native Regiments there were usually some Eurasian officers who had married native women and who were therefore well up in all native ways. One of these was usually put in charge of the catering, another took charge of the sheep club and livestock, a third looked after the wines and in this way everything was perfectly managed. Every year a pipe of Madiera was ordered direct from the island. This delicious wine was drunk in the Mess at little more than one rupee per bottle. The vines which produced this wine were all destroyed by the phyloxera and the wine made from the new vines is not a patch upon the old. Manilla cheroots were also imported direct and sold at an absurdly small rate.

In those days it was the custom if asked to dinner, even in the hottest weather, to dress up in red cloth shell jacket and sword, while a servant followed with a cool white jacket. On meeting your host he would inquire why you had come in a hot shell jacket, and knowing there was a cool one in reserve, he would ask you to go and change. Although this was the invariable rule, still it was considered *de rigeur* to make your entry in a red jacket.

Mian Mir was a very dreary station in those days, for there was no canal water as there is now for irrigation, and the barracks and bungalows were distributed over a barren plain with hardly any vegetation to be seen. The Church was the only home-like object. I was glad when it was announced to me that my name had appeared in Governor-General's Orders as posted to the medical charge of the 4th Regiment, Punjab Irregular Force, stationed at Dera Ghazi Khan. Nobody knew where this place was but they thought me lucky to get an Irregular Corps.

The first part of my journey was from Lahore to Mooltan, a distance of over 200 miles over a kutcha road which was little better in those days than a track through a jungle. I would have started this journey at the hottest time of the year in the end of July with only a wide-awake hat on my head if Mrs Jackson had not put a thick puggri[19] on it, besides furnishing me with sandwiches, a bottle of sherry and another of brandy for the road. I had to drive into Lahore and to start in the mail-cart from Ararkulli at the first streak of dawn. In the cool air of the morning the drive, although the cart had no springs, was exhilarating and my spirits were high. On we went at a gallop through the low jungle with the partridges calling and a black one (which I took for a grouse) every now and again getting up.

When we came to a watercourse crossing the track the driver would say, 'Hold on, sahib,' and over it we would go with a jolt fit to pitch me out, had I not held on by the iron railing. It was all delightful at first but, as hour after hour passed and the sun got hotter, my spirits began to evaporate and my bones to ache. I put up a rupee umbrella I had bought as an additional protection from the sun, but the iron handle got almost too hot to hold and my elbows got bruised by constant collisions with the iron rail. To add to my discomforts, my bottle of sherry got broken in crossing a deep nullah[20] and in trying to save some of it by drinking out of the broken bottle I ran the risk of mangling my nose. Towards afternoon we got a pair of hardly broken-in horses which fought and bit at each other all the way to the end of their stage. The driver as usual jumped out and removed the reins from the horses. He had scarcely done so when one of the horses made a bite at the other which gave a squeal and away they went at a tearing gallop along the road with me sitting helplessly in the cart and a poor syce hanging by their heads with his feet drawn up – so that at every step I expected to see him pawed down by the horses' feet. After a time I thought I would jump out and run to their heads and stop them – but my legs were so stiff and cramped that in trying to do so I fell before the wheel and the cart went clean over me from my shin to my shoulder. For a second I thought I was done for as I could not draw my breath and I thought my breast-bone had been crushed in on my backbone. But, after an instant, I felt I could breathe a little and gradually I got over it and crawled to the side of the road until the people from the station came up. The horses had fortunately come to a halt at a rising in the road two or three hundred yards ahead without injuring the syce and it was not long before we got fresh horses and went on again. This last adventure had taken it quite out of me and I refused to go on when we reached the dak bungalow at Chickawatni preferring to run the risk of not getting a seat the following night.

My 24 hours' rest here picked me up and, as the seat on the mail cart next morning was not occupied, I was able to go on, but I was so bruised and broken that I found the second part of the journey as trying as the first. The most of it was in the dark and the driver was always falling asleep, so that I often found the horses blazing along, with the reins lying loosely on their backs and whether they were on the road or not I could not tell. At last, about 2am, we reached Mooltan and I tumbled into my bed and covered my head with my clothes as I had a shivering fit notwithstanding the glass of Mrs Jackson's brandy which I had taken to keep it off. I stayed for some days with Dr. Macintyre, Civil Surgeon of Mooltan, to whom Dr. Curlang had kindly written to take care of me. I went to see the Fort in which are the tombs of Lieuts. Anderson and Agnew, who were murdered here by Moolraj, which atrocity led to the final annexation of the Punjab. Anderson was a Brechin boy and one of the big boys when I went to school. He was called 'Tangle' in those days because he was so long.[21]

On August 5th I left Mooltan and started for Dera Ghazi Khan in company with the Deputy Commissioner of Mozafferghur who had also been staying with Dr. Macintyre. I put up with him for the night and next morning I started at dawn to do the rest of my journey. Captain A. J. Wilde,[22] commanding the 4th P.I. had laid out horses for me and although I had difficulty in finding my way I at last reached the ghat on the Indus where boats were to be had for crossing to Dera Ghazi Khan, but this was owing to the horses' knowledge of the road and not to my guiding. I was very sorry to hear afterwards that one of the horses I had ridden had died on the road. The Indus was in full flood and we took a long time to cross it but at the other side I found a fresh horse awaiting me with a syce to show me the way. It was some miles to the cantonment and, as it was midday, the heat was great so I was very glad when we at last reached Wilde's house. He received me with a kindly welcome and said I must stay with him. He was a big powerful looking man and although under forty his baldness made him look quite that age. Captain Earle[23], second-in-command of the Regiment, was also living with him – a nice gentlemanly fellow, but without the necessary stamina for the rough life of a frontier officer. Lieutenant Paul was the Adjutant, a big, burly, rough-looking fellow with a bushy brown beard and hair cut very short. He was of a retiring and morose temperament.[24]

These were the only officers with the Regiment at that time. The other Regiments were the 2nd Punjab Cavalry, of which Captain Sam Browne[25] was Commandant (but was then at home on furlough), Lieutenant C. Nicholson[26], 2nd in command, Lieutenant D. M. Probyn[27], Adjutant, and Asst-Surgeon T. Maxwell[28] in medical charge. Also stationed there was No 2 Horse Light Field Battery with Lieutenant G. Maister and in command and Lieutenant Medley Rue. All these officers were but little known at that time, but in less than two years most of them had become distinguished and some of them even famous throughout Europe. There was a Garrison Mess at which all met at dinner and on my first night there they looked a free and easy lot compared with the Messes I had seen. Instead of being all in white starched uniform they dressed as they chose. Most were in soft muslin shirts with loose sleeves which, for greater cool-

Sir Sam Browne, 2nd Punjab Cavalry. Despite a severed arm and a smashed knee he killed an enemy gunner and won a VC during the Mutiny.

ness, some rolled up to the elbows, before beginning dinner. There was no formality about the speech used and much good-natured chaff was bandied about. One of them told a story in the course of which he alluded to some young lady as a 'heifer', where upon a usually reserved member said, 'How would you like your own sister to be called a heifer, Geordie?'; a remark which was received with applause by the others.

Most of the men had nicknames. Wilde was, of course, known as 'Jonathan', Paul as the 'Rooshian', Nicholson as 'Little Nick', his brother, the great Nicholson, being 'Big Nick'. They were a very happy community having their racquet court where they met every evening and their large public bath to which they afterwards resorted and where their bearers were awaiting them with clean clothes. They loitered there to get cool till the first bugle went for Mess, then dressed leisurely and went across to dinner. Their conversation at dinner was quite different from what would have been heard at Messes on the other side of the Indus. Instead of the usual local gossip it was mainly about matters connected with their Regiments, or about shikar,[29] or about the commotion that was beginning to arise in down-country Regiments on the introduction of the new greased cartridge into the Schools of Musketry. They all had their minds on their work, for none who was not a soldier at heart cared to remain on the Frontier, where the only excitement was a chance of a brush with the hill tribes.

Every Regiment was kept on a war footing ready to take the field at a moment's notice. Each had an establishment of mules to carry ammunition and water for the men; there were eight doolies, or one to each company, with 6 bearers to each and a sirdar and mate bearer to look after them in carrying the sick and wounded. Any number of camels could always be got to carry the tents, etc., etc. The men of the Regiment were from all the fighting classes – Sikhs, Pathans, Dogras, Punjabis, Mussulmen and Hindustanis (a few). They were armed with the Brunswick two grooved rifle and a sword bayonet, but many of the native officers and some of the men carried also their iron tulwar with a shield on their backs. They also carried a water bottle on service, the introduction of which caused some difficulty with the Hindustanis as they said it would destroy their caste in drinking out of them. They carried the bottles as ordered, without water in it, till Wilde insisted on them carrying the bottles filled, as he said if they did not care to drink it themselves it would be useful to others. They did not like to be made into bheesties[30] for the benefit of others and soon took to using the water themselves.

The men were divided into Messes of the different castes and religions and one or more cooks were allotted to each. Each Mess had a huge iron griddle on which the chuppatis, or big scones, were toasted while a large copper vessel (tinned) was used for cooking the 'dhal' (a kind of lentil) with which they ate their chuppatis. This arrangement led to great economy in carriage as well as leaving the men free for other duties. But the Hindustanis stuck to their habit of each being his own cook and for this purpose each man had to have his own lotah, or brass pot, to draw water as well as a large round brass dish for kneading his dough on and a small iron girdle for cooking chuppatis, with perhaps a flat stone and a roller to grind his 'mussalas' (seasoning materials). It can be seen what an amount of carriage and waste of time this entailed. Some of the Sikhs showed a desire to return to these Hindu habits when they thought they would not be noticed, but Wilde put this sternly down when he happened to come across anyone so occupied.

In those early days of the Force the officers were a happy bachelor brotherhood, there being only one married man, Captain W. Hughes,[31] commanding the 1st Punjab Cavalry. Besides his wife there were only two ladies on the Frontier, namely Mrs Graham, wife of the Deputy Commissioner of Dera Ghazi Khan and Mrs Cox, wife of the Deputy Commisioner of Bunnoo. The officers were all comparatively young men, only two being above the rank of captain, Major Cope[32] and Major Vaughan, (who got a brevet for service in the Crimea), They were all selected men and they remained select from the fact that the physically weak and those

Luther Vaughan, 5th Punjab Infantry, who commanded the Yusafzai Expedition in 1857.

who were not thorough soldiers at heart, or could not endure the isolated life, were soon eliminated from the Force. There was a strong clannish feeling among them; they all knew each other and most of them had nicknames. They thought nothing of riding 90 to 100 miles to pay each other visits, or for shooting or hawking parties. On one occasion Captain Keen rode from Dera Ghazi Khan to Peshawur in a little over three days to play in a cricket match and returned in the same way. Sam Browne would ride from one end of the Frontier to the other without thinking anything of it, and so did Lord Roberts in after years. Those were the 'copper-bottomed men' (to use a Chinese expression) whom John Lawrence loved.[33]

I had only been a fortnight in Dera Ghazi Khan when the Indus, which overflows its banks every year, came down in overwhelming force and burst through the earthen bund made to keep the inundation from the cantonments. Both officers and men turned out and tried to stop the breach in the bund and when that failed to cut a way for it through another bund. All was in vain and after two days incessant labour they returned to cantonments exhausted. The inundation slowly advanced on the Station and in the meantime bunds were being thrown up around the bungalows. Several officers returned with Wilde to his house to get some refreshment and rest. As I had not been of the working party I was told to watch until the water came into the verandah and then call them. It was a dreary vigil sitting on the verandah with the uncertain light of a lamp, watching the gradual approach of the inundation to the bungalow, listening to the fall of houses in the cantonments as they became sapped by water, for they were all built of only sun-dried bricks. As the water came near I could see by the dim light all kinds of small animals and creeping things crawling into the ruined verandah for safety. At last the water rose to the level of the verandah and about 2am I roused Wilde and the others. We all then made our way to the house of Lt. Medley, R.E.[34] which was situated in a higher part of the Station; doing which we had to wade through water above our knees. But in a few hours we had to leave this and make our way to

John Lawrence, a gruff and outspoken man, who was determined to restore order
ruthlessly in the Punjab.

the Native city which was built on a rising ground. We had to wade to that through water up to our waists.

We took up our quarters at the Kotwali,[35] the highest point of the town, where were congregated ever so many country people who had fled there for safety with their families, livestock and as much of their goods as they could carry. It was a scene of the most dreadful confusion, and to make things worse, a lot of rampageous ponies broke loose and went for each other, creating a perfect pandemonium for a while. The inundation gradually surrounded the town and although Wilde and his men toiled their hardest it burst through the bunds they had thrown up and drought down some of the houses in the lower part.

Arrangements had then to be made for a regular siege and Wilde did so by annexing all the grain and foodstuffs in the shops and giving receipts for it. He then went out in boats and rescued a lot of people who had taken refuge in the date palm trees which cover the country here (as well as at Mooltan), and which are supposed to have sprung from the date-stones left by the Greeks under Alexander the Great when he encamped his army at the latter place under one enormous banyan tree.

Some of the illustrated home papers of those times gave imaginary scenes of the inundation, representing groups of natives who had climbed the trees for safety along with a tiger and a snake. It was a very uncomfortable time for all.

The only room available in the Kotwali was occupied by the Deputy Commissioner, Lieutenant Graham, and his wife. We men had to be content with a thin sepoy's pall through which the sun's rays beat fiercely upon us. We tried to pass the time with chess and other games, but our brains reeled, and we had to run out and get more air by sitting under the meagre shade of a tree.

After many days of great discomfort the waters began to subside and we were able to return to cantonments and take up our quarters in one of the only houses that had not fallen down. When the water dried up it left mud with deep cracks, into which a walking stick would disappear, and which emitted a loathsome steam. We were devoured by mosquitoes and sandflies and all began to suffer from a low malarial fever.

It was a great relief when, about the end of September, orders were received for the right wing of the Regiment to march to Bunnoo. Wilde, Paul and I were to go on with it, and poor Earle had to remain with the left wing. I was sorry to say goodbye to him for I had taken a greater liking to him than for any of the others. I never had the luck to meet him again for he got an enlarged spleen from the awful fever that followed the inundation and had to leave the Frontier. It struck me so strange and unnatural, the cool way in which Wilde and Paul said goodbye to all the others with whom they had garrisoned for the past three years, for although I had only been a few weeks with them it was with a good deal of sadness that I said goodbye. However after a time I became as nonchalant at such partings as the others.

We left Dera Ghazi Khan on September 30th and Maister's battery accompanied us. As the country round was still more or less under water, and the road muddy and unfit for camels, the tents and other baggage were sent by boat for the first march and Paul and I went with them. Being a griff[36] I had made no arrangements for food and I found that Paul had only provided for himself. He had not forgiven me for not buying a horse of his for the march and kept himself to himself in another boat all the way. Fortunately the Eurasian bandmaster who was in the boat with me, seeing that I had nothing to eat, offered me some of his sandwiches. Then, at night, when my bearer tucked in my mosquito curtain round my bed, he handed me a round ball the size of an orange made of ghoor, parched ground grain and flour. I was glad of it and thought it very nice of my bearer to have thought of it. I was very hungry but too proud to beg from the Rooshian.

Next day we joined the Wing at a place not far from the river. I had bought a tent from the bandmaster and a pair of camel trunks with other camp equipage; Earle had lent me a horse and syce for the march, so I was now independent. My first night in camp, however, was not pleasant for my 3 camels had been squatted down in front of the door of my tent and the smell of them, with their abominable groans and gurgling, most effectively drove sleep from my eyelids. I enjoyed the marches very much for the cold weather was now beginning and the freshness of the early morning was delightful getting colder and colder as we advanced.

But the sickness in the Wing was very great; nearly every man in it having brought away a dose of malarial fever. It was miserable to lie at night and hear the poor sepoys groaning in fever and vomiting as if in cholera. And then I had no quinine except a small quantity which I had to reserve for the worst cases. The only thing I had to give the others was the bitter juice which my native doctor told me of, which he squeezed from the leaves of the jowasah plant, which grew everywhere over these desert plains and which he prepared every day. So every morning, when we arrived in camp, I paraded all the sufferers from fever and went round administering to each his morning cheerer of this nauseous green fluid. I don't remember the success of the treatment but at all events it let them see that they were not being neglected.

The road from Dera Ghazi Khan to Dera Ismail Khan is about 9 or 10 short marches. A young Engineer officer had determined to make it passable in all weathers and raised it considerably above the general level of the country. But the first rains bringing down the hill streams breached it in so many places that it became the most impossible part of the country to march over, especially for the battery that accompanied us.

It was interesting to watch how Maister got his battery over a deep nullah that one day crossed our path. There was a stream at the bottom of this and branches of bushes had first to be laid in it to prevent the wheels from sinking in the muddy bottom. Then long, stout ropes, manned by sepoys, were attached to either side of the gun carriage. Down the steep road, made for the carriages, the horses were then urged by their riders at top speed across the stream.

Stumbling and nearly falling among the branches they charged up the opposite bank as far as the impetus would carry them, but just when horses and gun were on the point of falling back, the sepoys with the ropes, who had scrambled after them as well as they could, would get into position and with a long, strong pull would land all safely at the top.

There was little variety in the marches from day to day but it became colder as we got farther north.

The band was a source of pleasure to us as it played for an hour in the evenings. For this we had to thank Wilde, the 4th being the only Regiment in the Force that had a band. Government refused to give a band allowance to the Punjab Frontier Force, but Wilde paid for the instruments himself, and we helped with the band-master's pay.

Another source of interest to me of an evening was watching the fires being lit and the men preparing for their evening meal. They were divided into Messes according to their caste or religion. To each Mess a cook was attached who kneaded the atta, or wheat meal, into dough from which the flat cakes called chupatties are made. They were then toasted on great iron griddles, carried on the march on mules. This is the common food of Northern India, seasoned with a sort of thin porridge made of pulse or lentil called 'dhall' and some-times supplemented by a little 'ghee' or preserved butter with high flavour, or with mustard oil in which some herbs or spices gathered from the fields have been cooked. The sepoys could rarely afford meat and yet what fine strapping fellows they were. Occasionally a few Sikhs would join their rupees and buy a fine old he-goat with a gamey flavour, discernible many yards off, which they considered the height of good feeding.

We reached Dera Ismail Khan and halted a day in that forlorn –looking station. In those days it was nothing but a few officers' bungalows and the mud huts of the sepoys dumped down on a wind-swept plain with not a tree or bush on it and in a perpetual dust-storm. Here was stationed one of the three Frontier ladies, the wife of Lieutenant Hughes, commanding the 1st Punjab Cavalry. We were in a dust-storm all the time we were at Dera Ismail Khan and at our first march out of it, at a place called Jarrick, there was such a hurricane that the tents could not be put up, except Wilde's single-poled tent which had been sent on the night before. It was ready for us and in it we officers huddled together all day long with our mouths and nostrils bound up with handkerchiefs to keep the dust out and unable to get any food cooked. Some bread and butter were got but the moment the cover was taken off the butter it became the colour of clay from the deposit of dust on it.

It was only at sunset that the hurricane moderated enough to admit of the tents being pitched. Our next camp was at the foot of the Sheikh-bu-deen, a rocky hill nearly 5,000 feet high, the sanatorium of the Derajal. It was delightful to be near a hill again and after breakfast I proceeded to climb a part of it. In the chinks of the rocks I found a beautiful sweet-scented flower like a mimulus which I was told was called 'the Prophet Flower'. But Wilde, when I returned to camp, told me I must never go wandering unarmed in these parts as prowling hill-men were often to be met; I thought I could have defended myself with the stones that lay about.

The following day we went through the Payzoo Pass and entered the Murwat Valley, which at this Season is nothing but bare sand but, in Spring, a sea of green grain. The inhabitants of this valley are a fine race, so different from those of the adjacent Bunnoo Valley, who are a truculent set of turbulent scoundrels living in fortified villages and always fighting among themselves. The difference in the appearance of the Bunnoo Valley and that of Murwat was quite as great as in the character of the inhabitants, Bunnoo being a land of trees and running brooks, with cultivation everywhere.

At Bunnoo, Paul and I were assigned quarters in the Fort at Dhulleepghur[37], but Wilde occupied a bungalow outside across the glacis of the Fort where the other officers and civilians were located. The Station Mess was also situated there and so unsafe was the place considered from the prowling robbers from the neighbouring hills that Wilde told off an orderly always to accompany me to and from Mess when I went to dinner.

Stories were then rife about in the Station about John Nicholson[38] who had been Deputy Commissioner there and had only recently been transferred to Peshawur. He had been a terror to evil-doers and was loved and feared accordingly. A ghazi from the hills had come down to gain glory in this world and endless joy in the next by murdering him. Nicholson was walking on the verandah of his bungalow with another man when the ghazi lifted the chik and walked in. Being puzzled as to which was his man, he called out in the hill language, 'Which is Nicholson? Which is Nicholson?' Nicholson having backed in the meantime towards the armed orderly always on duty at his house, seized a loaded rifle and presenting it towards the ghazi said, 'I am Nicholson Sahib and, if you advance a single step, I will shoot you dead!' The ghazi then stepped forward and instantly was shot through the heart. For all this Nicholson loved the wild hill men and when he left Bunnoo he placed a sum of money in the hands of the Civil Surgeon to be used every cold weather to buy warm clothing for the children from the hills who came in crowds with their parents for treatment at the Government Dispensary. This fund was at my disposal when I was Civil Surgeon during the winter.

I loved the cold weather at Bunnoo. It was so like home with its trees bare of leaves and its encircling hills covered well down with snow. My favourite walk was down to the Kurram River, about a couple of miles away, where a clear-looking stream reminded me of those I had fished in back in Scotland, while at the other side was a bare, uncultivated plain called the Wuzuri Thull, a dangerous stretch of country. On one occasion, after sitting dreaming on the bank of the river, I turned to walk back when I became aware that two hill-men were approaching with their jezails[39] slung over their shoulders. It was an awkward place to be caught in for they had only to cross the river to be safe in their own territory, so I thought the only thing to do was to put a bold face upon it and, straightening my shoulders, I walked towards them, keeping the middle of the road and in so doing making them separate as I came near to let me pass between them. I then walked for some distance without looking round, but all the time thinking I would probably have a bullet sent after me. When at last I did venture to look round I saw them swinging along towards the Kurram. They were fine looking men and handsomely dressed. I am sure they were none of the prowling robber tribe.

There was only the 3rd Punjab Cavalry, commanded by Captain Gill,[40] at Bunnoo when we arrived, but they were soon replaced by the 5th Punjab Cavalry under Lieutenant Paget.[41] The 1st Punjab Infantry under Major John Coke[42] shortly afterwards joined the garrison from Kohat. We had then a very jolly set of fellows and we had a pleasant time in the little while we were destined to be together.

Paget, generally called 'Billy', was great fun at Mess with the comical way that he told the story of some of the Frontier expeditions[43]. He afterwards wrote a history of the P.I.F. When he was stationed at Asnee, which is on the borders of Sindh, a heated correspondence on some subject arose between him and Colonel Jacob.[44] The Colonel always dated his letter from Jacobabad and Paget, having named a small outpost after himself, which he had established, and not wishing to be overawed by the sounding name of 'Jacobabad', was wont to address his replies from 'Paget-ka-Tool'.

Major Coke was a fine specimen of a Frontier officer – tall and dark with a handsome beard sprinkled with grey. He had raised at Kohat the 1st Punjab Infantry, which was composed chiefly of the Pathans of that neighbourhood, a wild, unruly lot that he kept in awe with a big stick that he always carried and with which he administered rapid and effective punishment. He was a simple man in his habits and was quite happy to eat from a chair in front of him his dinner, consisting of a fowl cooked and served by a Pathan khitmatgar[45] in a sheepskin coat. On these occasions he used metal plates with huge salt and pepper muffineers made of common tin. Coke's was a fine Regiment and the Afridi Orderlies in their rifle green uniform and high set puggries with a gold fringe hanging down the side of their head looked picturesque figures.

Our chief amusement was rackets and there was a splendid snipe jhil a few miles away. The country was not good for hawking, owing to the numerous water courses for irrigation, but we were not left to indulge in these sports for long, as about the middle of February 1857 we were ordered to join a Field Force under Brigadier-General Chamberlain[46] at Towsah, near Dera Ghazi Khan, collected to punish a tribe of Beloochis called 'Bozdars' who had given trouble by their raids. The march down was very pleasant. We had the 1st Punjab Infantry with us and Major Coke had his hawks which occasionally showed us some sport when he happened to flush partridges or a noubara from the patches of mustard we passed.

I forget if it was then or on some other occasion that Lieutenant I. Hughes of the 3rd Light Horse Field Battery had a very narrow escape of his life while going after a noubara. This smaller bustard is the principal bird which is hawked on the trans-Indus frontier. It feeds on the patches of mustard which occur here and there along this desolate land wherever the rare rainfall has accumulated and left a moist place. These places are hastily scratched by the native plough and sown with mustard seed. The green patches in spring afford a welcome relief to the eye from the all-pervading mud colour, and the scent from the mustard in flower brings memories of the fragrant fields at home. On such occasions you must keep your eye on the hawk and trust to your horse to avoid obstacles. This time Hughes' horse came suddenly on one of those ravines cut by the rain in the wide alluvial plains which are not seen until you are almost on their brink. Down horse and rider went, the horse being killed, but Hughes escaping without other injury than a peeled nose. As this organ of his was of unusual size we all declared it must have acted like a buffer and so saved him!

Lieutenant R. Mecham[47] commanded the battery. He was a remarkably nice gentlemanly fellow and an excellent draughtsman. Coke asked him to make a sketch for him of our desolate camp near Sheikh-bo-Deen. To make a better picture of it Mecham put in one or two palm trees but Coke refused to have it as he said they spoilt the sketch. Poor Mecham was murdered in his doolie the following autumn, between Bunnoo and Kohat, when on his way to Murree on sick leave.

We reached Towsah on March 5th and were joined there by the Left wing of the Regiment from Dera Ghazi Khan under Lieutenant R. P. Homfray,[48] formerly of the 17th Bengal Native Infantry, who had been posted to the Regiment. Poor Earle had been obliged to go away on sick leave.

A reconnaissance in force was first made to ascertain the position of the enemy at the Pass into their country, called the Khan Bund, in which a fine sepoy of Coke's Regiment was mortally wounded. Next morning, March 7th, we advanced to the attack on the Pass. As we approached we could see the enemy in their white clothes swarming on the hillsides. The 4th was ordered to attack the hill in the centre, and I remember, when we began to move off, a red-haired Pathan who had often amused us on the march by playing Scotch airs on a Pathan whistle, began to play 'Annie Laurie'. It sounded queer on such an occasion. The hill we had to climb was rugged and precipitous, but our men scrambled up in a kind of skirmishing order, and I made an attempt to follow them but soon found myself lost and evidently of no use in such a position. I returned to the bottom of the Pass where I found the other doctors had established a field hospital. I could see my Regiment gradually driving the enemy along the crest of the hill, aided by the shells of the battery, which were kept playing on the enemy in front of them. The 1st and 2nd Regiments were heavily engaged in other directions and the enemy were finally driven from the Pass and we encamped beyond it.

Our loss in killed and wounded was not great, but I remember it was quite as large as at the Battle of Mohmura[49] in Persia which occurred about the same time and of which so much was written, while ours was scarcely noticed. Only one officer was wounded, Major Coke, who got a bullet through the fleshy part of the shoulder.

The Bozdar[50] country, like all which lies among the Suliman Hills, consists of little but bare, barren, stony hillsides, though here and there a little cultivated ground is to be found which is irrigated by rivulets of water brought with great labour and skill along the hillsides, often from a great distance and sometimes by means of channels bored through the rocks. We encamped in one of these spots till the Bozdars submitted to the terms offered them. When we entered it looked a lovely green oasis in the desert with fields of growing corn, dates and other fruit trees sprinkled about. When we left it the crops had been eaten or trodden down, the trees had disappeared and the water-courses had been destroyed in many places. Such is the barbarous way in which war against the Frontier tribes has to be waged since there is no other way of punishing them if they choose to fly to their inaccessible fastnesses and refuse to submit.

Notes

1 John Lindsay Stewart was born in 1831 and studied medicine and surgery in Glasgow before joining the East India Company's Medical Establishment as an Assistant-Surgeon on 4 August 1853. He served at the siege and capture of Delhi in 1857 and became Chief Medical Officer of the Queen's Own Corps of Guides. He died with the rank of Surgeon-Major at Dalhousie, Scotland, in 1873. A keen botanist, he was the author of *Panjab Plants, Forest Flora Of North-West And Central India* and several other publications.
2 Kirk – died of heatstroke at Attock in 1857.
3 Charpoys – Indian bedsteads.
4 Ghurras – clay water pots.
5 Sunderbunds – known today as the Sunderbans or 'beautiful forest', these are a cluster of mangrove-covered islands stretching east from the mouth of the Hooghly River and in Fairweather's time heavily infested with Bengal tigers.
6 Munshis – a term used for Indian teachers and secretaries or general writers of letters.
7 Jhilmils – originally these were gauze blinds but later the term was also used to describe venetian blinds.
8 Dum Dum – the H.E.I.C. establishment here housed a major musketry depot but it also included a hospital.

9   Maidan – mid-nineteenth century arrivals at Calcutta were usually impressed by the sheer bulk of Fort William, the neo-classical scale of Government House, seat of the Governor-General and the expansive Maidan or 'field'. It had become the custom by the 1850s for Society to promenade on the Maidan at twilight. William Howard Russell, the war correspondent, was to complain in 1858 that this mingling of rich and poor in every kind of conveyance – sleek landaus, creaking bullock carts, fast carriages and oriental palanquins – was only enjoyable in the fifteen minutes before night fell. There are many good contemporary accounts of Calcutta. My favourite is Majendie, *Up Among The Pandies*, pp 23–55.

10   Sladen – this is Lt. William Sladen who joined the 81st Regiment on 1 June 1855.

11   Bheestie – an Indian water carrier.

12   Syce – a groom.

13   Punkas – or punkahs were large cloth fans hung on a frame from the ceiling and worked by pulling a cord.

14   Ranegunge – soldiers disembarking here in the 1850s found just a few miserable rickety wooden huts and various sellers of bric-a-brac and souvenirs at inflated prices.

15   Gharry – both Russell in his *My Diary in India* and Jones in his *Recollections Of a Winter Campaign in India* have splendid illustrations of these uniquely Indian modes of transport. Russell thought his looked like a baker's cart or laundry van – 'An inspection made it appear that there were slides which pushed aside, or opened out, and served as doors or windows. The traveller, when he has one to himself, gets his bed made, and stretches luxuriously at full length; for a spare cushion is made to fit the interval between the seats and beneath it is stowed some of the luggage. There are shelves and lockers at the ends of the vehicle, and – when it is well slung on the springs, and the four wheels are properly consorted – it is not by any means, apart from the question of the horses, an uncomfortable means of locomotion … the Indian traveller lives in his gharry, sleeps in it, and often eats in it.' (Russell pp 137). Captain Jones noted that a gharry made about six miles an hour allowing for stoppages. In his case the ponies were, 'not much bigger than cats', and the only way of starting, once the animals were in the shafts, 'was for half-a-dozen men to get hold of the wheels and shafts, and force the *crittur* on …' (Jones, p 25).

16 Dak bungalow – a post-house provided by the Government for travellers at intervals along major highways. Russell wrote: 'The bungalows, though varying greatly in actual comfort, are all on the same plan. A quadrangular building of masonry, one story high, with a high-peaked roof of thatch or tiles, projecting so as to form porticoes and verandahs. The house divided into "suits" of two, three, or four rooms, provided more or less imperfectly with charpoys, deal tables, and a very deteriorated tripodic and bipedal establishment of chairs. Windows more or less damaged as to glass and frames. Doors with perverse views as to their original purposes. Off each room, however, is that universal bath-room, and the earthen jars of cool water. The interior accommodations of the bungalows depend a good deal on their position. None are exempt from the visits of travellers – all ought to be ready to receive them, but in point of fact some are naturally much more frequented than others, in consequence of their situations being better adapted for halting. In some, the whole of the apparatus consists of a broken glass or so; a common earthenware plate; a knife, of no particular use in cutting; and a fork of metal, from which one or more of the prongs has lapsed. There are no napkins or tablecloths … The bungalow generally stands at a distance of twenty or thirty yards from the road, in an enclosure … The Government charges eight annas, or one shilling, to each traveller for the use of the bungalow whilst he halts.' (Russell pp 141–143). An additional cost was for food provided by the servants in charge of each dak bungalow. Dinner, almost by tradition and in the stories of countless Victorian travellers, consisted of a small and very tough chicken.

17 Mills – Robert Mills had joined the 9th Lancers on 8 October 1850 and left the regiment as a captain in 1859.

18 Doolie – a covered litter or stretcher; Europeans were usually carried long distances in them and it was the mode of conveyance for the sick.

19 Puggri – also spelled puggree or puggaree – a light turban formed of a thin scarf worn round a hat and sometimes hanging down behind as protection from the sun.

20 Nullah – a dry watercourse or ditch.

21 Anderson & Agnew – Fairweather is correct in his short allusion to events at Mooltan (Multan). After the close of the 1st Anglo-Sikh War in 1846 the situation remained tense throughout the Punjab and old Sikh dominions. Patrick Vans Agnew of the Bengal

Civil Service and Lieutenant W. A. Anderson, Bombay European Regiment, rode into Mooltan on 17 April 1848. Local feelings were at flashpoint. The two British officers were ostensibly there as an escort to the new governor, Sardar Khan Singh, but Vans Agnew, the senior of the pair, was under secret orders to drastically reduce the size of the Sikh army, much to the chagrin of its men. Vans Agnew was considered 'a man of much ability, energy and judgement', as 'the oldest political officer on this frontier' (Daly, *Memoirs Of General Sir Henry Dermot Daly* p 16). Anderson had served under Sir Charles Napier in his administration of the recently-acquired British province of Sind and was 'an excellent Oriental scholar' In a letter written en route Anderson described himself as 'a lucky fellow', but his good fortune ran out within 48 hours of his arrival in Mooltan. While inspecting a fortress on the morning of 19 April a soldier named Amir Chand suddenly attacked Vans Agnew with a spear, severely wounding him. Lieutenant Anderson tried to get away on horseback but was overtaken by some Sikh cavalry and received several sword cuts. The two officers were taken to their camp near the Idgah Mosque and that evening the helpless pair were murdered by a mob of local citizens and disgruntled Sikh soldiers. Their murder was the casus belli of the 2nd Anglo-Sikh War 1848–49. Further Reading :the best contemporary account of this period is in Edwardes: *A Year On The Punjab Frontier In 1848–49*, 2 vols, London 1851; on the actual murders the most detailed information can be found in Kohli: *Trial Of Diwan Mul Raj*, Patiala 1972; the situation at Mooltan is explored before, during and after the Sikh Wars in Roseberry: *Imperial Rule In The Punjab 1818–1881*, New Delhi 1987; a good source on the political background is Mahajan: *Annexation Of The Punjab*, New Delhi 1949; the two best general accounts of the Anglo-Sikh Wars from a military point of view are probably Gough & Innes: *The Sikhs And The Sikh Wars*, London 1897 and Bruce: *Six Battles For India*, London 1969.

22   Wilde – the son of a rich solicitor with aristocratic connections, Alfred Thomas Wilde was born at Kirby Cane Hall near Bungay, Suffolk, on 1 November 1819. Educated at Winchester School he obtained a commission as ensign in the East India Company's army on 12 December 1838 and joined the 15th Madras Native Infantry, quickly transferring to the 19th Madras Native Infantry in June 1839. Apart from some minor disturbances on the Malabar coast, Wilde had an uneventful eleven years with his regiment, but

his language skills probably helped his appointment as adjutant
of the 3rd Punjab Infantry in 1850. Within days of transferring to
the 4th Punjab Infantry, as second-in-command, in April 1851, he
was leading men into action against Waziri tribesmen in the Kohat
district and defeating a night attack by them upon the fort of
Bahadur Khel. This soon led to his promotion to brevet captain with
full captaincy on 23 November 1856. Fairweather thus met Wilde
on the eve of his brilliant career as a North-West Frontier fighting
soldier. His achievements, post-Mutiny, are detailed in note 1, p 203.

23 Earle – he had joined the 4th P.N.I. from the 24th Bengal Native
Infantry on 30 April 1856 and due to sickness did not officially
leave the Regiment until 16 January 1858.

24 Paul – it is clear that, despite his undoubted bravery, this officer was
not liked by Fairweather whose description of him and his moods
is unique; he had transferred from the 7th Bengal Native Infantry
on 29 September 1854.

25 Browne – inventor of the Sam Browne belt, worn by generations
of British officers – this brilliant cavalryman had been born in
India in 1824, entered the East India Company's army in 1840 and
saw action at the battles of Chillianwallah and Gujerat (Gujarat)
in the 2nd Sikh War. He served with the Punjab Cavalry from
1850–69, principally as commandant of the 2nd P.C. His attack on
an enemy gun battery, despite a sword cut that severed his left arm,
won him the Victoria Cross on 31 August 1858 against mutineers
at Seeporah. He commanded the 1st division of the Peshawur Field
Force during the 2nd Afghan War 1878–80 and was made a full
general in 1888. He died on 14 March 1901. There are tablets to
his memory in St Paul's Cathedral and also in Lahore Cathedral.
<u>Further Reading</u>: Browne, *Journal of the Late General Sir Sam
Browne*, Edinburgh 1937.

26 Nicholson – born in 1831, Charles was the favourite younger
brother of the celebrated John Nicholson. He had arrived in India
in 1846 and it must have come as a shock when the two brothers
met in February 1847 in Lahore where John arrived after trekking
through massive snow drifts in the mountain passes of Kashmir
following a reconnaissance along that frontier. Charles had been
only ten years old when his brother had left England. One of
the most delightful anecdotes in Fairweather's manuscript is the
nicknames of the Nicholson brothers. One wonders if anyone ever
dared call the fearsome John 'Big Nick' to his face!

27 Probyn – born in 1833, Dighton Macnaughten Probyn joined the
    Bengal Cavalry in 1849 and rose quickly to become one of its most
    famous soldiers. He served along the trans-Indus Frontier 1852–57
    but it was his prowess in countless actions during the Indian
    Mutiny that cemented his fame. In fact he took part in so many
    personal combats outside Agra, fighting enemy cavalrymen with his
    sword, that he was awarded the Victoria Cross. After the Mutiny he
    saw more action in the 2nd Anglo-Chinese War 1860 and Umbeyla
    Expedition 1863 before being made an equerry to the Prince of
    Wales in 1877. This led to a new career as an important member of
    the Royal Household. Laden with honours, he lived beyond the 1st
    World War and died at the age of 91 in 1924.

28 Maxwell – born on 6 November 1823 and educated in Glasgow,
    Thomas Maxwell qualified as an Assistant Surgeon in 1846 and
    served in four battles during the 2nd Anglo-Sikh War. During the
    Mutiny he was to see more action at the Relief of Lucknow, the
    Rohilkand campaign and was wounded at Mohanpur. He retired
    from the Army in 1868 with the rank of Surgeon-Major.

29 Shikar – a term used to describe hunting as a sport.

30 Bheesties – also bhisti or bheesty – a native water carrier.

31 Hughes – a fine cavalry officer, William T. Hughes was the last
    'commandant' of Hodson's Horse and rose to become a general.

32 Cope – I have included this spelling as used by Fairweather but
    it is, I think, clearly a typing error in his manuscript and refers to
    Coke, of whom more later.

33 I think Fairweather is here getting a little confused between the
    two Lawrence brothers, Henry and John (there is a third, George,
    but he does not enter our tale). The 'Paladins', as the leading
    Frontier soldiers and administrators became known in the years
    1846–57, owed much more to their mentor, the kindly, deeply
    religious Henry Lawrence, rather than to his stern younger brother.
    These Frontier warriors were often called 'Henry Lawrence's young
    men'. Further Reading: Allen, *Soldier Sahibs*, London 1999, a lively
    account of some of these men and their doings; there are numerous
    references to the goodness of Sir Henry Lawrence but the gruffly
    serious John had many critics, e.g. Ricketts, *Extracts From The Diary
    Of A Bengal Civilian*, privately published, 1893.

34 Medley – an officer of the Bengal Engineers, Julius George Medley
    wrote an account of his experiences on the Bozdar Expedition
    and in the Mutiny (including being garrison engineer at Lucknow

during the siege) in *A Year's Campaigning In India*. He later rose to become a major-general.

35 Kotwali – an Indian police station, though it can also refer to a magistrate's court.

36 Griff – the shortening of 'griffin' which, in Anglo-Indian parlance, always meant a newcomer. The origin of the term is obscure and some writers concluded it may have been used to denote 'a raw Welshman'. India was a land of such mystery and surprises for the newly arrived Briton that the griffin was always a source of fun. Further Reading: Bellew, *Memoirs of a Griffin*, London 1843.

37 Dhulleepghur – the fort, placed in a high position overlooking the river and valley at Bunnoo (Bannu), had been built by Herbert Edwardes, another of Lawrence's young men, at the close of the 1st Sikh War. For a detailed account the reader can turn to Edwardes' own account in *A Year On The Punjab Frontier*.

38 Nicholson – born on 11 December 1822 into a family of strict Ulster Protestants, the eldest of four boys who would all die in India, John arrived as a cadet in the Bengal Army in 1839, just in time to take part in the invasion and subsequent disastrous retreat from Afghanistan. These events were swiftly followed by the Anglo-Sikh Wars and the legend of Nicholson as a fearless administrator of the Frontier districts was soon born. He managed to convey to an extraordinary degree – as Fairweather points out in his anecdote – a mixture of fear and loyalty among the tribesmen. At the Siege of Delhi in 1857 Nicholson was the driving force in planning the final assault. His death during the entry to the city made him a saint in the pantheon of Raj heroes. To some, such as a young Frederick Roberts, the tough Nicholson was the beau ideal of a soldier. Others, then and since, have wondered if he was not a little mad. The man who was worshipped as a living god by some tribesmen was also the same man who wrote during the Mutiny to his old friend, Herbert Edwardes, Commissioner at Peshawur, 'Let us propose a Bill for the flaying alive, impalement, or burning of the murderers of the women and children at Delhi. The idea of simply hanging the perpetrators of such atrocities is maddening ... I would inflict the excruciating tortures I could think of on them with a perfectly easy conscience.' (Hibbert pp 293). Further Reading: the standard Victorian biography is Trotter, *The Life Of John Nicholson*, London 1897, and the best modern hagiography is in Allen; for a different view of him see Hibbert and also Thompson, *The Other Side Of The Medal*, London 1925.

39 Jezails – the long muskets used by North-West Frontier tribesmen; it is interesting that Fairweather notes these guns were slung over the shoulder in the same way that modern Pathan (or Pashtun) warriors carry their infinitely more deadly and sophisticated weapons.

40 Gill – a simple error, I think, on Fairweather's part; the officer he refers to was J. S. *Gell.*

41 Paget – William H. Paget was later commanding officer of the 5th Punjab Cavalry.

42 Coke – the 7th son of a country parson, John Coke left for India in 1827 and joined the 60th Bengal Native Infantry, later transferring to the 10th B.N.I. He saw no action until he transferred again to the Bengal Irregular Cavalry in time to fight in the 2nd Sikh War at Chillianwallah and Gujerat. He was fortunate in making the powerful friendship of Sir Charles Napier, Commander-in-Chief of the East India Company's Army, and also Sir Henry Lawrence. In May 1849 Lawrence invited him to raise the 1st Punjab Cavalry. It was said that by 1858 he had seen a decade of continuous action. During the Mutiny, as a dashing leader of cavalry, Coke and his men saw countless stiff fights. Later he returned to England and became High Sheriff of Hertfordshire, finally dying at the age of 91.

43 Expeditions – here Fairweather is slightly incorrect; Paget never wrote a regimental history of the Punjab Frontier Force, but he did co-author the first exhaustive history of British campaigns on the North-West Frontier. Further Reading: Paget & Mason, *Record Of Expeditions Against The North-West Frontier Tribes*, London 1884.

44 Jacob – another unbending hero of Empire, John Jacob was born in Somerset in 1812. After studying at the East India Company's seminary at Addiscombe, he sailed for India in 1828 and a cadetship in the Bombay Army. It was the 1st Afghan War that pushed Jacob's career forward and he gradually became noticed as an administrator and political officer of importance. Baluchistan, at the southern end of the Frontier, was the area where he really made his name and he was a progressive thinker on all thing military, especially the use of Irregular Horse regiments and the treatment of native soldiers. He was very proud of founding the town that still bears his name and his own regiment, Jacob's Horse. After service in the Persian War 1856 and holding the southern frontier steady during the Mutiny, Jacob died in December 1858 and was buried at his beloved

Jacobabad. Further Reading: Shand, *General John Jacob*, London
1900 and Lambrick, *John Jacob of Jacobabad*, London 1960.

45   Khitmatgar – also khidmatgar, khidmuttgar, etc. – a butler, waiter or,
in Raj terms, often a personal manservant.

46   Chamberlain – one of the least assuming, largely forgotten and yet
important Victorian soldiers, Neville Bowles Chamberlain was born
in Rio de Janeiro in 1820. His father was Consul-General for South
America. Family connections got the young Neville a cadetship
in the Bengal Army and he arrived in India in 1837. He seemed
to be in the thick of fighting throughout the 1st Afghan War
1838–42. The following year he was seriously wounded in action
at Maharajpore during the Gwalior campaign and more battles
followed in the 2nd Sikh War 1848–49. On 13 December 1854
the Governor-General, Lord Dalhousie, nominated Chamberlain
to take command of the recently formed Punjab Irregular Force.
He had already led two expeditions against the Orakzai Afridis
and one against the Turis in the Kurram Valley when the Bozdar
Expedition was mooted. Subsequently Chamberlain was to be one
of the heroes of the Siege of Delhi bringing his Moveable Column
from the Punjab. His reward was a step up to Adjutant-General of
the Bengal Army. After the Mutiny he led more frontier expeditions
culminating in the bloody Umbeyla Expedition against the fanatics
on the Black Mountain in 1863. More than a decade later he was
supposed to lead a diplomatic mission to Kabul but the refusal of
the Afghans to receive Chamberlain and others led to the start
of the 2nd Afghan War. He died a field-marshal in 1902. Further
Reading: Forrest, *Life Of Field-Marshal Sir Neville Chamberlain*,
London 1909.

47   Mecham – this gallant officer met a sad fate at the hands of Kabul
Khel Waziris in 1859: 'On the night of 5 November of that year,
Captain R. Mecham, Bengal Artillery, commanding No. 3 Punjab
Light Field Battery, was proceeding from Bannu towards Kohat,
when about two miles from the outpost and village of Latamar,
he was set upon and murdered by a gang of marauders. Captain
Mecham was at the time very ill and was travelling in a doolie; his
escort consisted of two sowars of the Bannu mounted police, he
having sent on two men of his battery to Latamar to increase his
escort from there. It does not appear that the murderers had any
previous knowledge of an officer being likely to pass that way; they
were simply prowling about on a marauding expedition, and seeing

the approaching light of the torches, they had hidden themselves in some bushes to waylay the travellers. The moment the attack was made, the mounted police basely deserted Captain Mecham, and the doolie bearers took to flight. Captain Mecham attempted to keep off his assailants with his revolver, but he was overpowered and cut down.' (Paget & Mason p 474).

48 Homfray – he joined the 4th P.I. from the 27th Bengal Native Infantry on 7 November 1856 but, as related by Fairweather, was to die on 16 September 1857 from wounds received on the previous day.

49 Mohmura – the last battle of the Anglo-Persian War 1856, and therefore remembered as its climax, Mohammerah (to use its other name), was certainly a bigger victory politically than militarily (it was also very much a naval action). British casualties including wounded were just 41; Fairweather is thus right in his assessment of losses since in the attack against the Bozdars the British lost 5 killed and 49 wounded. However, enemy losses were estimated at 300 killed and wounded at Mohammerah, while the wily Bozdars lost 20–30 killed and 50–70 wounded. Further Reading: on the Anglo-Persian War the best contemporary account is Hunt, *Outram And Havelock's Persian Campaign*, London 1858 and the best modern re-telling is English, *John Company's Last War*, London 1971.

50 Bozdar – this expedition is covered in the Introduction to this book but for a full appraisal the reader is directed to Paget & Mason pp 604–614.

2

Outbreak of Mutiny – 55th N.I. Disbanded – Yusafzai Expedition

The Bozdars caved in and there was no more fighting, so we went back to our several stations. We had not long settled at Bunnoo when the news of the outbreak of the Mutiny at Meerut on May 10th, and at Delhi on the 11th, 1857, reached us. Homfray was then staying in the Fort with me and he was horror-stricken when he read the names of those who had been massacred at Delhi, for it was said he was engaged to one of the ladies then mentioned. We had made preparations for settling down for the hot weather, but now it was felt there would be no rest for us. First the 1st Punjab Infantry was ordered off down country and we feared we were to be left behind, but in a few days we also got orders to go by forced marches towards Lahore. We started on May 24th, our places in the Fort being taken by the Field Battery while a squadron of the 5th Punjab Cavalry, under Lieutenant G. Younghusband,[1] accompanied us. As our men marched out of the Station a large number of the Bunnoochis were watching and some of them called out, 'You'll never come back here again.' They were mistaken, for the

1st Sikh Infantry from Dera Ismail Khan were already on the march to take our place.

We crossed the Indus at Esa Kheyl and a tedious business it was to get the great, awkward, long-legged camels into the boats. Their feet sprawled everywhere but in the right direction and some of them were so obstinate that their legs had to be tied under them as they knelt on the ground so as to roll them like casks down the bank and over planks into the boat.

While we were lying on a high bank watching the embarkation there was a sudden rumbling and movement of the bank as if it were falling into the river. We took to our heels, but it turned out to be a slight earthquake, and no damage done. When I got myself across I mounted my horse and made for the camp as it was then about mid-day and very, very hot. The track at first lay through the sand by the river and a pariah dog that was following me began to whimper and yelp as if in pain. While I was wondering what could be the matter with the brute, he suddenly threw himself on his back, holding his paws up in the air and licking them to cool them. He continued to do this every now and then till we got off the sand. After this we only marched in the night, starting at sunset, and halting at midnight for half an hour's rest. The ground was often so hot as to be unpleasant to lie down on it.

The country was a roadless desert and a guide had to be got from village to village. Water for drinking had to be carried with us, and the men who had objected to the water bottles were glad of them now. The water was not always of the cleanest, but in the dark it passed muster. On one occasion I was glad to avail myself of a sepoy's water-bottle. I was to have drunk in the native fashion by having the water poured into my hand, so as not to contaminate the vessel by putting my mouth to it, but the sepoy, knowing that it would not be observed by his fellow caste-men, told me to drink in my own way.

In one of these marches our rearguard chanced to come across the rearguard of a Hindustani Regiment which was being sent out of the way of mischief to Dera Ismail Khan as we afterwards heard.

Some of these Hindustanis spoke to our men and said what a fine opportunity it was to kill their officers and go down to join the mutineers at Delhi!

We reached Kushab on the Jhelum on June 1st after a very trying march. It was a very long one and the tracks across the plain so indistinct and confusing that our advances and rearguards were constantly going astray and the bugle call, 'I've lost my way', sounded all night long, delaying our progress. Sunrise found us wearily trudging on almost in single file or in groups. I noticed some of the men walking along half asleep like drunken men and actually making feeble attempts at fanning themselves. At last the gleam of the sun on the Jhelum made us believe we were near our camp, but we found we had still 3 or 4 miles to go, and we straggled into camp, one by one, dead beat. Nearly half the Regiment did not come in at all but remained all day in villages or huts they had come across and were brought in at night, many of them on bullocks and donkeys by the people of the country, so done up that they could not walk. A little dog of mine disappeared the same night and never turned up again.

We had to halt here to rest the men and the camels. While doing so a despatch was sent down the river ordering us to proceed towards Attock instead of continuing on to Lahore. This was a great disappointment to all and we commenced our march up the side of the Jhelum with little enthusiasm while the squadron of cavalry went on to Lahore. We marched by Pind-Dadan Khan across the great Salt range to Chukowal. When we were here encamped and were lying half asleep in our tents we were suddenly alarmed by the sound of a native drum being beaten in the camp. In those times the idea of mutiny was always in our minds, but it turned out to be only a challenge from the Police Battalion there to a friendly bout at wrestling. We accepted the challenge and had to go out and sit in the hot sun at mid-day to watch the proceedings, wearing our pistols, as we were never sure how these things would turn out. Our man, though not so powerful as the police champion, was more active and a better wrestler, and in the end downed his opponent. At this there was a great outcry and the beaten man rushed up to Wilde and declared he had not been properly thrown. But Wilde said it was a fair throw, patted him on the shoulder and gave him something to heal his wounded vanity.

From here we made our way straight across country to Wah on the Grand Trunk Road near Hassan Abdal. It was through a countryside without roads and so broken up with ravines that we had often to wend our way through them in single file while the camels had great difficulty in following us. They were wearisome marches. Wilde frequently remarked how easily with his Native Regiment he could tire out and baffle any British Regiment in such a country and in the hot weather. Wah was one of the halting stages for the Mogul Emperors on their annual migration from Delhi to Kashmir. Some of the ruins still remain and the clear running streams looked delicious to us after the dry country we had come through, as doubtlessly they had also done to the old Moguls and their harems. We got a mahseer here for our dinner, the best I ever tasted, no doubt owing to the clear water in which it had lived.

From Wah we marched by the Trunk Road to Attock, where I put up with my old chum Kirk, then in medical charge of the garrison. At that season Attock is a veritable oven; the black rocks absorb so much heat during the day, which they give out again at night, so that there is no relief from it all. The temperature that night at Mess was 107° Fahrenheit. It was with a shock, though not with wonder, that I heard of poor Kirk's death from heat apoplexy, not long after we passed through.

We crossed the Indus at Attock in boats on June 17th. It was almost startling how rapidly the boats shot down the river when they were let go. The boatmen pulled at their oars with all their might, but it seemed doubtful whether they could prevent the boat from being carried down through the narrow gorge in the rocks. However, they shot into a back current at the other side of the river and, as if by magic, we were quietly floating back towards our starting point, but on the opposite side.

From there a short march took us to Nowshera which was to be the limit of our journey for the present, (the distance marched from Bunnoo was 353 miles in 23 days). This Station had recently been flooded by the Cabul River near which it stands and most of the officers bungalows had been destroyed. We were obliged, therefore, to take up our quarters in some sergeants' houses which had escaped the flood, being made of bricks. The 55th N.I. had been stationed here, but had been sent to Hoti Mardan when the Guides went down country. They had mutinied there and fled into the hills. Here they were hunted down and killed or brought as prisoners to be blown away from guns. Their mutiny so affected their C.O., Colonel Spottiswoode,[2] that he committed suicide.

Ensign J. W. McQueen[3] of the 27th N. I. Was posted to us and joined soon after we reached Nowshera. At that time stationed there were a wing of the 27th Foot and the 10th Irregular Cavalry, the latter regiment being well known to be only waiting its time to break out into mutiny. A few days after our arrival a parade was ordered and the men of the 27th and we of the 4th Punjab Infantry had our rifles loaded. The men of the 10th Cavalry were dismounted. As they came on parade a Company of our men marched into their lines and took possession of their horses, etc. On reaching parade they were at once ordered to lay down arms. Seeing it was hopeless, they did so without a murmur, and were marched down country under an escort of wild Pathan horsemen, recruited by Lieutenant I. B. Lind, 5th Punjab Cavalry. On July 1st Paul and McQueen left with a detachment.

On the outbreak of the Mutiny, orders had been received by all regiments of the Force to recruit up to 12 Companies, but we had been unable to do much in that way at Bunnoo. At Nowshera, however, we had crowds of applicants. Every morning I had a long row of them to select from and the best men were easily picked out. There was one little Pathan who appeared morning after morning but was always rejected for no other reason than his size. At last, Wilde asked him if he could get any recruits in his own country, Yusafzai? He would only promise to do so on condition that he himself were enlisted because, he said, his example would induce others to follow it. Being anxious to recruit from that part Wilde reluctantly engaged the little man and sent him off to his home. Soon he returned bringing some strapping fellows. It may be mentioned that he turned out a first-rate soldier, though his size was always something of a blemish in the ranks. He went with the Regiment to Hindustan, got his ankle smashed by a ball in an engagement, and was eventually discharged on pension.

The life at Nowshera became very monotonous. The little bungalows were like ovens, the temperature, even in the morning, being over 100°. I developed a constant low fever which made every exertion a labour. Even going and coming between my quarters and hospital each morning became a great effort. On my return I threw myself on my hot bed quite exhausted and not wishing to move for the rest of the day. I had no desire for food, except a perfect craving for acid fruit, which I satisfied by devouring peaches and grapes brought from Peshawur. I would certainly have fallen into some severe illness had not the Regiment got orders to march to Hoti Murdan to join an expedition against a village in Yusofzaie called Narinji. Here a lot of mutineers and Hindustani fanatics[4] had collected. The lethargy that had crept on me at once disappeared. To get to Murdan we had to cross the Cabul River and march 10 or 12 miles and, as it was on July 17th, in the hottest time of the year, it was intended to do it in the night.

We went down to the bank of the river in the evening, but owing to some difficulty about boats, did not even begin to cross till 8am next morning. We had, therefore, to march through the heat of the day and only arrived at Murdan past mid-day. The heat was sometimes suffocating and once, on crossing a small nullah on the road, I suddenly felt as if I would choke. Digging my spurs into my horse, I rushed up the opposite bank, where I was able to breathe again. I have been exposed to many hot suns since then but never felt so near a sunstroke.

On reaching Murdan I at once went into a cold bath to take the heat out of me, which it did effectively, for my fingers began to be pinched with cold and my teeth to chatter. I realized I was in the grip of an ague fit, the first I had ever had (but not the last), and it was quite pleasant for a time to feel cold once more after weeks of roasting.

After a day's rest the Force, under Major Vaughan[5] of the 5th Punjab Infantry, moved out against the village, but the heat was so intense that out of 800 men composing the column, more than 40 were struck down by the sun, of whom 9 died. Wilde and 14 of our men were so struck. Poor Wilde was unconscious for hours and was sent back to Murdan. Homfray was the only officer with the Regiment at the attack on the village as I was left behind in charge of the Hospitals. Narinji occupies a strong position in the mountains of the Yusofzaie border and had successfully withstood several Sikh attacks. Our attack on this occasion was only partially successful. I was told that Vaughan was so afraid of exposing his Regiment (the 5th P.I.) too much that he never made a serious assault. Homfray, with our men, carried half the village and had he been supported he said he could have cleared it out, but he was recalled and Major Vaughan decided to wait for reinforcements. On the arrival of these I believe he carried the village, but in the meantime we got orders to march to Delhi. We had lost in this futile attack a Native Officer, a Non-Commissioned Officer killed and 8 men wounded.

Notes

1 Younghusband – this gallant young officer was killed in action at Khudaganj on 2 January 1858 – the same action that saw Fred. Roberts win his VC – and had until then led something of a charmed life. During the battle at Agra he was on horseback when he and his mount both fell 50 feet down a well. Two more horses and their riders then fell down on top of them. Luckily for Younghusband, he had fallen in a sitting position and his horse fell standing and across him. The animal took the full weight of

the other two horses and their riders, who were all killed, but Younghusband suffered only a few bruises!

2   Spottiswoode – he had for many years been adjutant of the 21st Native Infantry. His length of service with the 55th is unclear; contemporaries such as Cave-Browne and Kaye say just a few months, yet based on his service record, examined by Saul David, it was two years. The usual inference is that despair drove him to his death, a melancholy mood brought on by watching his regiment being broken up, a hurt pride and shame. He certainly told anyone who would listen that he had 'implicit confidence' in his men. Luther Vaughan saw things differently and felt that Spottiswoode was 'disgusted' with his men and hurt that they had been driven to mutiny by a foolish British officer. In his memoirs Vaughan wrote: 'This sad news was confirmed by a letter found on the Colonel's table addressed to me. In this letter Spottiswoode reproached me as being the cause of the mutiny of his regiment and his consequent suicide. Of course he referred to the forcible removal of his guards at Attock. The letter was painful reading because Spottiswoode had been a brother officer, and very much my friend in earlier days; but my instructions were imperative, to place my own men in charge of the bridge as promptly as possible. The hesitation of the sepoy guard to give over their post when formally called upon to do so by my officer, looked, under the circumstances of the day, very like mutiny.' Vaughan felt that the 55th N.I. would probably have mutinied anyway and he was only following orders. Yet, in hindsight, he confessed: 'On looking at the matter through a long vista of years, I am free to admit that a little more patience on the part of my officer would not have been out of place, and that at least he might have referred them to me (for I was close at hand), to resolve their scruples as to giving up their post.' (Vaughan p 74).

3   McQueen – along with Alfred Wilde, John Withers McQueen was the most famous officer whose career was forged in the 4th Punjab Infantry. He was born in Calcutta on 24 August 1836, son of a chaplain, educated in Scotland, and returned to the land of his birth with a cadetship in the East India Company's army, serving first in the 27th Bengal Native Infantry before transferring to the 4th P.I. Fairweather details several instances of young McQueen's heroism and he was recommended – unsuccessfully – for the Victoria Cross for his brave actions at Delhi and Lucknow. After the Mutiny he served with the 4th P.I. in campaigns against the Kabul Khel Waziris

in 1859 and Mahsuds in 1860. In April of that year he became second in command of the Regiment while still only a substantive lieutenant. In 1870, with the rank of captain, he was appointed to command the 5th P.I. and remained with them until 1883. In the Jowaki Expedition 1877–78 he was mentioned several times in despatches. Roberts selected McQueen and his Regiment to serve with him throughout the 2nd Afghan War including both invasions of Afghanistan, the siege at Sherpur and famous march to Kandahar. A year later he led his Regiment against the Mahsuds and was appointed an a.d.c. to the Queen and a full colonel. In October 1886, after many years on the Frontier, he was made Commandant of the Punjab Frontier Force. This honour was tarnished by the Black Mountain Expedition 1888 in which he commanded with the temporary rank of major-general; Roberts, then Commander-in-Chief in India, felt that the objectives of the expedition had not been reached because McQueen had listened too much to the advice of his political officer, contrary to his own warnings and advice. Brutally, when McQueen gave up the P.F.F. command in 1891, Roberts made it clear that he would not recommend him for any more appointments. He retired back to England and was promoted to lieutenant-general in 1895. His eldest son, Malcolm, was killed during the Boer War. He died on 15 August 1909 and was buried at Wimbledon.

4   Fanatics – followers of Syed Ahmad Shah, born 1786, and by all accounts a remarkable lookalike of Osama Bin Laden. This Sufi mystic and the fundamentalist philosophy he preached were to be a thorn in the flesh of the Raj. He made his appearance on the Yusafzai frontier in 1823 with just 40 followers preaching strict wahabi doctrines. Soon he had more than 900 fanatical adherents all willing to die for Allah in a jihad against the infidels. The Sikhs tried unsuccessfully to root out these Wahabi fanatics but they had made a stronghold of the Yusafzai district and especially the wooded and precipitous Black Mountain. From 1853 onwards the British had to send expeditions against the Hindustani Fanatics; others followed in 1857 (as detailed by Fairweather), 1858, 1863, 1868, 1888 and 1891. Further Reading: Wylly, *From The Black Mountain To Waziristan*, London 1912 is one of several histories of frontier expeditions, other good ones are Nevill, *Campaigns On The North-West Frontier*, London 1912 and Elliott, *The Frontier 1839–1947*, London 1968; for a superb interpretation of wahabi

fanaticism and its effect on the Raj see Allen, *God's Terrorists*, London 2006.

5   Vaughan – born in 1828, J. Luther Vaughan (he never used his first name), joined the 21st Bengal Native Infantry in 1842 and stayed with them until 1850 on transfer to second-in-command of the 2nd Punjab Infantry, P.I.F. Shortly afterwards he transferred again, to the Regiment for which he was forever associated, the 5th P.I. In later years it would become the 58th, Vaughan's Rifles (Frontier Force). While recovering from illness in 1854 he offered to lead a contingent of Turkish troops to fight in the Crimea. He was back in India and the 5th P.I. again in time for the Mutiny and the events described by Fairweather. Apart from the Yusafzai affair the 5th were retained in the Punjab and had little chance of glory. That came in abundance six years later in the Umbeyla Expedition where Vaughan distinguished himself in several hand-to-hand combats with fanatical ghazis. Not long after he resigned in disgust at what he thought was a stagnating career. In 1878 he became a war correspondent and one of the few to serve with Roberts' army in southern Afghanistan and the Kabul to Kandahar march. Further Reading: Vaughan, *My Service In The Indian Army – And After*, London 1904.

3

March to Delhi – Storming of the City

We rejoiced in getting away from these piddling skirmishes to the real seat of war. We went back to Nowshera on July 28th when four companies of the Regiment were transferred which, with four companies from the 8th Police Battalion, were formed into the 20th Punjab Infantry, which afterwards became a famous Regiment under Colonel Brownlow.[1] The transfer of these four companies was a very difficult matter for Wilde, since he naturally wished to take his best Native Officers with him, as he was going on service. But he did not think it would be fair to transfer only the indifferent officers. It took him a deal of trouble before he finally arranged it all and the NCOs selected to go with the four companies felt it terribly as it seemed almost a disgrace to be removed from the Regiment when it was going down to Delhi, (long afterwards Brownlow told me he was not at first pleased with some of the NCOs Wilde had sent, but that one of them turned out his right-hand man and all the others turned out well).

The events of the march to Delhi I will describe from a letter sent home by me from Lahore. Wilde, Homfray and I did not accompany

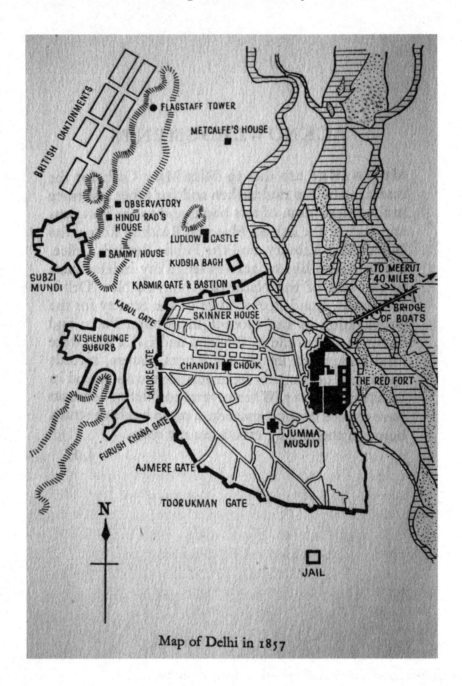

Map of Delhi in 1857

the Regiment on the first leg of the march, but remained behind to settle up accounts and rode out in the evening to camp, where we had dinner by moonlight, no tents having been put up.

Started 12 o'clock the same night for Attock but had to remain there for a day owing to a provoking delay having occurred in bringing over the camels. At 5 pm, August 2nd, we started for Hassan Abdul (30 miles), but on reaching a small river half-way we found it impassable from the rains. We lay down to sleep on the bank in the hopes it would have fallen by the morning. But while we were breakfasting and just preparing to cross a tremendous rain came on and filled it from bank to bank. Our tents, pitched in a hollow place between the hills, were nearly carried off by the torrent that came thundering down before they could be removed. It was provoking to be thus delayed by such an indifferent stream, but we had to curb our impatience till it fell next day (4th), about 2 pm. We then commenced our march – very hot for an hour or two – reaching Hassan Abdul about 9 pm but held on to make up for lost time. At midnight we halted for two hours and had a dinner of cold meat and tea. Then to sleep. We cursed the bugle when it roused us, being quite certain that we had only been asleep exactly five minute, then trudged on till sunrise, when we encamped.

That day we tried to sleep, had an early dinner and started again at sunset, reaching Rawalpindi next morning. It was a steaming hot day there and as I looked up at the hill station of Murree I could not help envying my friends, Earle and Thorn, who were vegetating in the cool breezes there. We halted here three days by order and then went on to Jhelum in two long marches, but through an interesting, broken, hilly country, looking beautifully green at that Season, and so not so wearying as in our previous marches. After reaching camp at Jhelum heavy rain fell and made the tents so heavy that we were unable to begin crossing the river till next day (10th), about 3 pm, intending to march on from the other bank. But here again a provoking delay occurred by some neglect on the part of the overseer of the ferry which prevented all being got over till late at night.

Two marches brought us to the Chenab, which we crossed next morning, and just had time to pitch our camp when another downpour came on. This again prevented us marching at sunset, as we proposed, but we stole a march of 12 miles next morning when the sun was overclouded and started in the evening a long one of 30 miles to make up for the delay. As we passed the battlefield of Gujarat[2] a Sikh in the ranks remarked that they had got a good hammering there and now he was going down to fight for us. We put up at the house of Mr. Cripps, Deputy Commissioner, built by Harri Singh, an old Sikh Sirdar, in a fine garden.

Another torrent of rain prevented us marching at night as we intended. Camp presented a most wretched appearance – the tents being all surrounded by water and everything wet and uncomfortable. Next morning (15th) it looked very unpromising, but fortunately a breeze sprang up, soon drying the tents, so we determined to march at once, in spite of the sun, and accordingly got under way about 12 o'clock.

It was hot and steamy at first, but another storm with thunder and lighning came on, without any rain where we were, and the sky remained clouded, so that we had a lovely march. I say lovely because it was the first march we had had in the middle of the day and everything looked so fresh and green while we also were so fresh ourselves after our previous night's rest. The 20 miles did not look in the least long. We had got to within 2 miles of our camping ground, where we intended to dine and, after a few hours rest, go on again the 14 miles to Lahore, when we met a horseman who told us the road further on was impassable for camels. Wilde, however, determined to proceed, but we soon wished he had not, for we came to the most horrible grief. During daylight it was possible, by great care and giving the animals as much time as they liked, to get most of them through the mud. But no sooner did the sun set and night come on than one after the other the camels slid and fell in the mud. Here they lay and refused to budge. There was no help for it but to spend the night in this puddle for the country on either side of the road was a sheet of water. One has to make the best of things on these occasions so, selecting the best paddled path through the mud, I wrapped my blanket round me and lay down with the men and animals splashing past my head.

I actually slept, for after a time Wilde came and roused me, as he and Homfray had managed to get a charpoy to sit on. I had never laid three in a bed before, nor did I think it possible to do so on a charpoy, but I know that we three managed to sleep soundly for some time lying across the bed and our feet in the mud! We had sent on word to the place where we had intended to dine so the khitmatgar brought the grub to us. He did not arrive till three in the morning and, when we awakened, found our coverings soaked through with the heavy dew, although we had been very jolly and comfortable under them. Being sharp set after our long fast, we shouted for the victuals, but to our sad disappointment, only a dry loaf with no butter and a cup of bad tea made with half-boiling water was produced. We could have skinned the khitmatgar alive but, in reality, it was not his fault, for he had expected all the dinner things to come and had brought nothing along in the panniers on his mule. As soon as daylight came the bugle was sounded and everyone set to work extricating the camels and baggage from our slough of despond. It was now a little drier and everything was got out by 9 am. Soon we reached our camping ground, which was barely two miles beyond this beastly snare, but a fine march was thoroughly spoiled.

We reached Lahore (14 miles), on August 17th, about mid-day, after a brutal march; the rain had begun soon after we left our camping ground and came down in such torrents that we were obliged to halt on the road and to sit there like statues on our horses for two mortal hours meekly waiting till it should blow over. We reached the Ravee at 9 am and occupied ourselves in drying our clothes and getting some breakfast till our camels and baggage came up. On crossing the river we encamped for the day, but next day (18th), we moved up to a position near the city and crowds of people turned out to see us. The impression must have been good, and they must

have wondered where these new Regiments came from, so differently dressed and so different in appearance from the old Hindustani
Regiments. To add to the troubles of the march from Nowshera,
Wilde had not thoroughly recovered from the effects of his sunstroke, which was followed by an outbreak of boils all over his body
and a frequent tendency to dysentery. He had therefore often to be
carried in a dooly.

I also suffered from fever which had to be constantly starved
off by quinine. In some of our long night marches I had once or
twice seen a sepoy staggering along asleep but I never supposed for
a moment supposed a European could do this. However, one night
after passing Rawal Pindi, I was so overpowered by sleep that I constantly had to get off my horse and walk for fear of falling off. On
one of these occasions I must have been going along asleep for I
suddenly roused by coming bump up against something and finding
a horse's head over me. Having been challenged by a Native Sowar
in an insolent kind of manner as I passed his post, I at once thought
we had been attacked by mutinous Cavalry and was grappling with
the man to pull him off his horse when I perceived from his long
gray beard that he was a Sikh, and at the same time he exclaimed,
'Sahib!' in rather an astonished way. I believe he also was asleep
when the collision took place, I found afterwards he was an orderly
of Sir J. Lawrence on his way to Rawal Pindi.

We were to have left Lahore on the evening of the 18th but as
Sir J. Lawrence[3] wished to inspect the Regiment we had to remain
another day. He also gave the men a feast in recognition of their
good conduct and decorated five of them with the Order of Merit[4]
for distinguished gallantry in the Bozdar and Narinji affairs.

We marched the same evening well knowing we were the last
Regiment Sir John could send to Delhi. We reached Amritsar on
the 20th and were there joined by the detachment under Paul and
McQueen which had been sent off from Nowshera to join General
Nicholson's Moveable Column. They had taken part in disarming
the 58th Native Infantry and 2nd Company of the 14th Native

Infantry at Rawal Pindi, and joined in the pursuit of the 14th Native Infantry mutineers at Jhelum, and of part of the 26th Native Infantry mutineers near Amritsar. It was at Amritsar we caught the cholera which was prevalent there and carried it with us to Delhi. Men were sometimes seized by the disease on the line of march and died soon after being carried into camp. On reaching Phillour we found the Breaching Battery had been got ready to take down to Delhi. We accompanied it as a guard till we were close to Delhi when it pushed on ahead and arrived there before us. When we got to Karnal, 30 miles from Delhi, we began to hear the sound of the guns. The cannonade seemed so constant that we were afraid the place would be taken before we got there. Homfray, who had all along been in a nervous state of mind to reach Delhi, and who had always been urging Wilde to push on at all hazards, could stand it no longer. Imploring leave to go on in advance he rode straight in from Karnal.

The boom of the guns was the first sign of our being near the seat of war but, as we went on, the signs became more and more apparent; the road strewn with deal camels and oxen, the stench from which was horrible; blackened and ruined villages which had been destroyed by our troops for maltreating the wretched fugitives from Delhi; branchless trees; ruined and gutted bungalows, etc., with a constant passing to and fro of armed men, camels and laden wagons. General Nicholson came out to meet us and there was a great turn out to see us as we marched into camp with band playing and colours displayed.

A nice place had been prepared for us near the other Punjab Regiments. Soon our tents formed a new street in the canvas city. After breakfast I went off to find my old friend and school companion, Dr Lindsay Stewart, in medical charge of the Guide Corps with which he had been on its celebrated march and all through the Siege. I had difficulty in finding out where the Guides camp was and, mistaking my way, went up a small hollow towards the Ridge, which I afterwards heard was known as the 'Valley of Death' from the number of round shot that fell into it from the city walls. I should certainly have avoided it had I known, although I believe no one was ever really killed there.

On reaching the summit of the Ridge a feeling of emotion came over me as I saw the city spread out before me with its long line of walls and bastions and realised that I was now in the presence of a great siege, such as I had often pictured, but never expected to see. While I was standing there beside my horse a Goorkha⁵ sepoy came sauntering slowly along the Ridge with his hands behind his back. He was the image of unconcernedness. I tried to find out from him where the Guides were located, but he either did not understand my language or did not take the trouble to do so, for he merely said, 'Mujho malum nahin – mera Nankari uddar hai,' ponting towards Hindoo Rao's House, and then sauntered away as leisurely as before. He had not gone more than 20 or 30 yards when a puff of smoke appeared from the city wall followed, to my no small surprise, by a round shot pitching on the road mid-way between the Goorkha and me. The latter took no notice of it, nor did he increase his pace, while I made the best of my way down the Valley of Death again.

I visited our old Bunnoo friends, the 1st Punjab Infantry, but found great changes among them. Coke again hors de combat with a bullet through his thigh; Travers, his second-in-command, killed and also (Billy) Lumsden⁶ who used to amuse us so much on the Bozdar Expedition; the loss among the men too had been heavy. Till the day before our arrival no attempt had been made to take up positions between the ridge and the city; then a strong body of skirmishers had been sent down to clear the ground and prepare for the breaching batteries. This was done almost without loss although the whole of the ground was covered with trees, bushes, walls and ruined houses. We expected to have at least our first night in bed after arrival, but I got orders to accompany a party of 350 men who had been ordered to commence a battery only about 200 yards from the Water Bastion – a thing said to be unparalleled in war.

After dark we moved quickly down the road towards the Kashmir Gate and turned off the left into the Kudsia Gardens making our way with as little noise as possible to the place where the battery was to be erected. For a long time the enemy seemed unaware of our presence so near them, and continued to fire an occasional roundshot towards the Ridge as usual, the deafening sound of their guns telling us how close we were to them. But at last some noise attracted their attention and a charge of grape was sent in our direction. As it crashed through the trees over our heads, I heard one of the men say to another, in an awed whisper, 'Graf hoga' ('That will be grape'). They had never been under the fire of big guns before. As the sound of the pickaxes and men at work increased the enemy opened a heavy fire of grape and musketry upon our position and casualties began to occur. Some of our men were wounded while working with the pickaxe and shovel. When their injuries were being dressed they would say to me, 'Sahib, we don't mind being killed or wounded as soldiers, but we don't like it when working as coolies.' Whereupon I had to dilate a little on the dignity of labour.

I had to remove my hospital to the shelter of a neighbouring ruin and while walking backwards and forwards I met another officer and fell into conversation with him. After a time he said, 'Is your name not Fairweather?' When I said indeed it was he said, 'And I am Fandy.' He was a young Royal Engineer who had come out with me round the Cape only 18 months before. A few days afterwards he was one of the first victims to fall at the assault.

When daylight came well in the enemy discovered what we were about and came out in large numbers, skirmishing among the bushes, trying to drive us out while a fire from the wall was kept up incessantly. During this fighting I could not but admire the way in which some of the 60th Rifles took advantage of every bit of cover to keep the enemy at bay. One man in particular got up on a ruin and from behind a chimney or broken piece of wall kept up a constant fire on the enemy in the garden until at last he was shot through the arm and came to me to be have his wound dressed as there was no surgeon of his own Regiment present. It was, fortunately, only a flesh wound.

The work and skirmishing went on without intermission till 1 o'clock when another party came down to relieve us. We retired feeling more and more comfortable as we got out of the reach of the shot. Our loss on this, our first night at Delhi, was 2 killed and 3 wounded, one of the killed being a jolly Pathan who had amused us on the way down. When I went to call and report myself to the Principal Medical Officer in camp he was very glad to hear that I had been down in the trenches since the Commander-in-Chief had been inquiring why no surgeons had been ordered down there.

We were again sent down to the trenches on the 9th and 10th, but were more lucky on these occasions – none being killed and only 5 wounded, One fellow got a whack in the rear from a spent grapeshot, which knocked him on his face and made him roar as if he had been badly wounded, but there was no greater injury than if he had received a good kick in the same quarter. On the 9th, when we were at the house called Ludlow Castle, guarding the battery erected on the 8th against the Moree Bastion, a strong body of cavalry, infantry and some field pieces came out towards us and we expected a fight. As they approached the big guns ceased for a little time, during which they were being charged with grape and turned on the enemy – then bang, bang, bang, and when the smoke cleared away, no enemy was to be seen. After this, we were having some breakfast, spread on a stair behind the house that led up to the roof, and out of reach, as we supposed, of shell being fired from the city. Suddenly a shell burst exactly over our heads and a triangular piece fell with that nasty fluttering sound right in among us, but only smashed some dishes. In a short time after the erection of the battery against the Moree Bastion it was reduced to a heap of ruins. But on the top the rebels had the cheek to place a field gun, which was, of course, at once sent flying by the big guns.

The battery against the Kashmir Gate was opened on the 11th and, of course, was masked until ready to be opened. I was on the top of the Observatory to watch it. When it commenced, with a grand salvo from all its guns at once, we saw the smoke followed immediately by the red dust from the impact of the shot, and the enemy flying in all directions for their lives – all before the roar of the guns reached us. A mortar battery was also opened on the 11th to throw shells into the Palace to intimate to His Majesty that the avenger was at his gate. It was curious that three of Dr. Guthrie's apprentices were present at the Siege of Delhi: Dr. D. Scott, medical storekeeper; Dr. I. Lindsay Stewart, in medical charge of the Guides, and I; while Dr. Martin Lamb was with some Irregulars in the neighbourhood, and two others were engaged in the Mutiny in other parts of India – Dr. Alex. Guthrie and Dr. W. G. Don, both of the British Medical Service. There was also in camp Dr. Sinclair Smith of the 9th Lancers who was my predecessor as Assistant to Dr. H. S. Anderson of Selkirk

The work was so constant and everyone was so occupied during the week before the assault that I had no opportunity of making many acquaintances among the Regiment there. Of all the Regiments that came under my notice I thought the 60th Rifles, the 9th Lancers and the 1st Bengal Fusiliers were the smartest and least affected by the length of the siege. The Rifles were always to be seen where work was to be done, clean and active; the Lancers were also as smartly dressed as in cantonments and ready to volunteer for any service. If a Horse Field Battery passed I often saw that some of the men were Lancers. The two officers who were most talked about in camp were General Nicholson and Hodson.[7]

The pounding of the breaching batteries were so incessant, both day and night, that by the 13th it became evident that the assault would soon be practicable. On that night a party of Engineers, of whom Medley of Dera Ghazi Khan garrison was one, crept down in the dark to examine the breach, and from their report it was decided to make the assault the following morning. That night I accompanied Wilde on a visit to Coke who, being wounded, was unable to lead his Regiment at the assault and was living in a bungalow down near the city. I shall never forget the scene that presented itself – the lightning-like flashes, the smoke and deadly roar of the guns, the rain of shells like falling stars and the streams of musketry fire from the walls all seemed like a dream of something I had read about rather than a reality.

On our leaving Coke said to Wilde, whom he loved like a brother, 'God keep your old head, Jonathan.' On return to camp the order had been received for the assault in the morning and preparations were being made. Fearing I might run short of bandages I sacrificed a new night shirt to add to my supply. About midnight we were paraded and told to fall in at the Gorge (a cutting through which the road to the Kashmir Gate passed). Here we remained while the orderlies and staff officers rode backwards and forwards giving orders and arranging the columns till the approach of dawn when we began to move slowly forward. As daylight came we were near the city wall and then all at once the guns in the batteries ceased firing, the skirmishers dashed forward with a cheer to keep down the musketry fire from the walls, and while one column assailed the main breach, another headed by Salkeld and Home of the Royal Engineers advanced to blow open the gate.[8] This was done with the loss of so many gallant men. The column then passed through and met the other column, which, in the meantime, had carried the breach.

The 4th Punjab Infantry was in what was called the 'Reserve Column'. But there was no such column for it followed the rest through the gate and joined in the fighting inside, advancing on the College, which they cleared of the enemy and held for the night, after barricading the verandah facing the Magazine with sandbags.

All doctors were left at a house established as a field hospital outside the city wall. Soon a stream of doolies bringing the wounded, dead and dying began to arrive so that we had no time to think of anything but our duties. As the doolies came in I was always afraid to open the purdahs in case I should see the face of one our officers but I was spared such a shock on that day. When any of our wounded men arrived I always asked about our officers and the reply was that they were all doing well. The sepoys evidently admired young McInsen[9] the most for they said he was' a bahut atchcha jawan' and a 'khub feringhi'. I will not describe the scenes in the General Hospital, but will merely mention that my friend, Sinclair Smith, who was a keen operator, was in his element. He not only performed his own operations, but offered to operate or assist any of the other surgeons, and at last became so exhausted that he had to throw himself down on a charpoy and lie there until the next doolie arrived, when he would jump up as keen as ever.

One artillery man, an Irishman who required amputation of the arm above the elbow, seemed in rather a jocular spirit over it. He was not sure about taking chloroform but submitted; when all was finished and the arm covered up by a towel he was roused and sat up. He was asked if he would now like his arm to be removed to which he gave his consent. The towel was then taken away and when he saw the arm off, and everything done up, he said, with a grin, 'Well, Doctor, it's the best piece of work I have ever seen and I'll have to stand you a drink for it!'

It was a sad sight to see the great Nicholson lying in one room mortally wounded through the lung and his brother Charles, with his arm amputated, in another room and both asking how the other had fared. The truth was kept from both of them as long as possible.[10]

I have kept one memento of that day in the shape of a ball from a wall piece that smashed the thigh bone of a very fine Pathan sepoy of the 4th P.I. For which I had to amputate at the hip joint (my first amputation).

The loss of the Regiment on this, the first day of the assault, was 3 men killed and 2 NCOs and 22 men wounded. Although the medical officers did not share in the immediate dangers of the assault, there was the risk that the enemy might issue in force from the Lahore Gate in order to make a counter-attack on the flank of our assaulting columns and, seeing that our attack on the Lahore Gate was driven back with loss, there only remained the 9th Lancers between us and such a mishap. The Lancers had been placed in this position as none of the infantry could be spared. It was a fine sight to see how coolly they circled their horses under the very walls while the assault proceeded. On that first night our spirits were not high, for although we had got inside the city we had only succeeded in holding a small corner of it between the river and the Moree Gate, while our losses had been great. Our right attack on the Lahore Gate had been repulsed and, worst of all, General Nicholson had been mortally wounded.

So depressed was the Commander-in-Chief, Archdale Wilson,[11] that it was said he actually talked of retreating, but Nicholson, when he heard this said, 'Thank God I still have strength to shoot him if he should venture to do such a thing!'

On the 15th I went into the city to search for the Regiment and found it occupying the College, which had been barricaded with sandbags against the musketry fire from the Magazine, which was only a short distance in front of them. Wilde was there at the back having made an orderly room, as usual, with his pipe in his mouth and his band playing just as if he had been in cantonments, regardless of the crash of the mortar battery close by, throwing shells into the Magazine and Palace, together with the roar of cannon and mus- ketry all round. He even had the band with him the previous night and when the sound of it reached some of the European Regiments nearby they thought at first it proceeded from the enemy's lines, but when they knew it was the 4th P.I. Band it had a cheering effect.

During this day, (15th), while some of our men under Homfray were holding a street they were attacked by a body of the enemy and poor Homfray was mortally wounded. He was taken to the Moree Gate where I found him under the care of Mrs Tyler,[12] (the solitary lady in camp), whom he had formerly known. He told me at once that his wound was mortal. He feared the bullet had come acciden- tally from one of our own men since, as soon as the enemy came down on them, the European Regiments that held the street farther back began to fire promiscuously into them. It was sad to think such was the case and I hope he was mistaken. He calmly asked for paper and, having dictated a short Will, he signed it with a steady hand

Archdale Wilson, the cautious general who defeated the Delhi mutineers.

and I had him carried to my tent in camp across the Ridge where I remained with him all night till he died.

Next day (16th) I was the only mourner at his funeral in the graveyard where so many of the brave now rest who died before Delhi. The Rev. Mr. Rotton,[13] Chaplain, read the service over him.

I felt his death much being the first officer we had lost and having lived with him. He was a good fellow although his colour was a little dark.[14] On this day the Magazine was stormed by the 4th P.I. And the 60th Regiment with but little loss as the enemy bolted as soon as the breach was won. The rest of the Force were also advancing their positions by degrees and fortifying as they went. This continued day by day. More and more of the city fell into our hands.

One day I took it into my head to visit the most advanced position and found there a European, dressed in common clothes with a double-barrelled rifle, sitting quietly at a loophole in the barricade. A number of men of a Balooch Regiment from Bombay were firing away as hard as they could, but the European said he did not know what they were firing at as he had not been able to see a soul. I had heard of a man who had lost his wife and children by the mutineers and who had taken an oath to revenge them. It was said he infested the advanced position and that many of the enemy had bit the dust from his patient, determined stalking. I cautiously mounted the barricade to look over and as I did a bullet whizzed close to my ear. When I came down the man said quietly, 'That was for you,' and I believe it was!

By the morning of the 20th most of the town was in our possession but the Palace still held out. McQueen was then on picquet near it with 40 men and took it into his head to go and have a peep through a crack in the gate. He saw several guns trained on the gate but no men apparently inside. On reporting this to Colonel Jones[15] a gun was sent to blow in the gate; McQueen at the head of the men passed in, but as he did so he got a shot through his helmet from a mutineer who at once rushed on him. McQueen told me afterwards that although he carried his drawn sword in his right hand, and his revolver in his left, it never occurred to him to make use of either. Instinctively he used his fist (holding the sword) and knocked the fellow down where he was dispatched by the men. In this affair McQueen's conduct was brought to the notice of Sir A. Wilson.

On the same day Lieutenant Aikman, attached to the Regiment, with a party of men captured the Selimghur Fort, the last position in the city held by the enemy. When I heard that the whole city was in our possession I determined to go down and see what was going on, although an attack of ague was just coming on me, so I swallowed a dose of laudanum to ward it off and rode down with my old friend Stewart to the Kashmir Gate. As we went along we met crowds of natives from the city, chiefly women and children, passing out under our protection. At the Kashmir Gate those leaving Delhi were examined by the guard to see that none of the mutineers were allowed to escape in this way. As Stewart and I were going through the Gate a man having the cut of a sepoy was being examined by the guard. He had told them he belonged to the Guides. Wherupon Stewart asked him if he knew who he was, but the man was unable to name him, so he was detained.

We made our way towards the Palace. The beautiful Diwan-in-Am had been used as a hospital by the mutineers and the poor inmates who had been unable to fly had been ruthlessly butchered in their beds when our men entered. It was the general belief that the Palace would be blown in the air to mark our abhorrence of the massacres committed there. Wishing to save a flower made of different coloured precious stones from the ornamented walls and pillars, I tried to scoop one off with my knife, but it went to pieces in the doing, so I tried no more. I have often thought myself a Goth for having done this. I would never have done so unless I had supposed the whole place was to be destroyed.

From there we were taken by a young officer to the 'Tochi Khana'. It had not been previously entered and was filled with all kinds of valuables – elephants howdahs and trappings, guns and rifles in cases, Kashmir shawls and clothes of all kinds used for native courts. I can't remember a tithe of the things. I might have loaded myself up, but was forbidden by the orders issued as to plunder. However, I took an anklet lying about as a memento and had it made into two muffineers which I still use today. Nothwithstanding the strict orders about looting[16] I saw some officers high in the service stowing away a silver hookah as I passed through one of the halls.

As Stewart and I returned to camp by the the Kashmir Gate the guard were still searching everyone for loot as they passed out of the city and a whole pile of things of all kinds and descriptions lay in a promiscuous heap by a wall. Whether they ever reached the prize agents I doubt, for the next day I saw it looked like a rubbish heap which had been gone over by rag-pickers, and one of the guards was rummaging to see if he could find anything of value in it.

I had not much time to go through the city after this, so can't say much about the scenes of desolation which no doubt existed, but I was kept busy with my wounded and preparations to go off on further service with a column to be sent off after the mutineers under Colonel Greathed.

A sad occurrence was the sale by auction of the deceased officers' effects. Poor Homfray's things, among others, were sold and I bought his concertina which he had often played when we lived together at Bunnoo. It beguiled many a weary hour for me during my first period of service in India and accompanied me in all my wanderings till my retirement.

Notes
1   Brownlow – Charles Henry Brownlow was born in 1831 and arrived in India as an H.E.I.C. cadet in 1848. In May 1851 he was appointed adjutant of the 1st Sikh Infantry and served with them in the Hazara campaign 1852–53 and in operations against the Michni Mohmands in 1854 and Bozdars in 1857. It was in April of that year Sir John Lawrence selected Brownlow to raise an 8th Regiment of Punjab Infantry. This became more famous a short time later as the 20th Punjab Infantry (Brownlow's Punjabis). The regiment saw action in

many frontier campaigns and in 1871 Brownlow was appointed to command the Chittagong column of the Lushai Expeditionary Force. When a general he became the Duke of Cambridge's resident expert on Indian affairs at the Horse Guards. Regimental records state that 5 native officers, 37 NCOs and 108 men from the 4th Punjab Infantry formed the nucleus of the new 8th P.I. along with 266 native officers and men from the 5th P.I. <u>Further Reading</u>: Anon, *History Of The 20th (Duke Of Cambridge's Own) Infantry*, Devonport 1909.

2   Gujarat – After two bloody and bitterly contested wars the Sikh kingdom of the Punjab was finally won by the British at the Battle of Gujarat, 21 February, 1849.In the six-hour engagement the British lost a surprisingly low 96 of all ranks killed and approximately 700 wounded. Sikh losses were considerably higher. Lord Gough, the British commander who liked using his infantry and was famous for his maxim, 'At them with the bayonet!' had at last learned the lesson of the dreadful Battle of Chillianwallah in the previous month and Gujarat was largely won by the British artillery. See Bruce pp 298–320.

3   Lawrence – John Laird Mair Lawrence was born on 4 March 1811, five years after his equally illustrious brother, Henry. Unlike the rest of his brothers, who had gone to Addiscombe, the training college for the East India Company's army, John was sent to Haileybury to be schooled for the Indian Civil Service. Both brothers arrived in India in 1830 and, after studying for and passing various language exams, John chose to work in Delhi. Soon he became an important revenue officer in various parts of the North-West Provinces. His gradual rise through hard work led to the key post of Acting Resident at Lahore in 1846 at the close of the 1st Sikh War. John was therefore in a key position to influence the course of events and extend British influence. From 1853 he was Chief Commissioner of the Punjab and watched over the fledgling Punjab Irregular Force. In the Mutiny he made a tough business of running the Punjab and was ruthless in crushing any hint of revolt, yet he was also a conciliatory Viceroy 1864–69, working to improve relations between British and Indian communities. A strong opponent of the Forward Policy on the North-West Frontier, he died in 1879 during the 2nd Afghan War. John was tough, uncompromising, deeply religious and as blunt as any old soldier. He worked long hours and expected others to do the same; one member of the N.W.P. Civil Service wrote that, 'We had few things

to be thankful to him for, and from him to us the thanks were not forthcoming' (Ricketts p 4).

4 The Order was the Victoria Cross of the Indian Army; it consisted of three classes and was distinguished by a badge in the shape of a star with the inscription, 'Reward for Valour'. The first awards had been made following the taking of the fortress at Ghuznee in Afghanistan in 1839. The men decorated on this occasion were sepoys Mir Afzal and Gulab Singh for the Bozdar Expedition, Havildar Makmad and sepoys Jehangir and Muhammad Bakhhsh for the Yusafzai Expedition. Further Reading: Hypher, *Deeds Of Valour Of The Indian Soldier Which Won The Order Of Merit*, Simla 1925.

5 Goorkha – the Sirmoor Battalion of Gurkhas, commanded by Major Charles Reid, were given the task of defending Hindoo Rao's house. This lay on the far right of the British lines. Further Reading: Reid, *Extracts From Letters And Notes Written During The Siege Of Delhi In 1857*, London 1861.

6 Lumsden – Billy was the brother of the much more famous Harry Lumsden, founder of the Queen's Own Corps of Guides, the most pukkha of all the Indian Army regiments and Punjab Irregular Force. Having served in both Sikh Wars, Harry Lumsden began a life-long association with the North-West Frontier. The Guides had been formed in 1846, at the behest of Henry Lawrence, who saw the need for a highly mobile force of native infantry and cavalry to police the new frontier. Lumsden remained a champion of the Punjab Frontier Force right up to his death in 1896. John Nicholson wrote to Harry on 1 September 1857, to say: 'Your poor brother was killed at the head of his regiment in action on the 25th. He died nobly doing his duty, and sincerely regretted by the whole army. His last words, as he fell dying to the ground, were ones of encouragement to his men and officers.' (Lumsden & Elsmie p 212). Further Reading: Lumsden & Elsmie, *Lumsden Of The Guides*, London 1899.

7 Hodson – the most controversial British figure in the Mutiny was William Raikes Hodson,, brilliant irregular cavalry leader and hero to many, crook and cold-blooded murderer of princes to others. Born in 1821, he reached India in time for the Anglo-Sikh Wars and soon carved out a reputation as a brave soldier. It was while in the camp at Delhi that Hodson, serving with the 1st Bengal European Fusilers, was allowed to raise a regiment of cavalry that, on his death, took his name. All might have been pure lustre but Hodson is

forever associated with taking under arrest three sons of the Mogul
Emperor, Bahadur Shah, stripping them naked and shooting them
at point-blank range with his Colt revolver. This was condemned
at the time and ever since (see Dalrymple as just one example), but
Hodson's biggest critic was the Victorian historian, Thomas Rice
Holmes, who in a scathing 26 pp appendix to his history of the
Mutiny summed him up as 'a splendid leader of irregular horse, but a
most unscrupulous man.' (Fifth edition, p 616).

8   Gate – both Salkeld and Home were officers of the Bengal
Engineers, both were awarded the Victoria Cross for their
outstanding heroism and, sad to relate, both died soon afterwards.
<u>Further Reading</u>: Perkins, *The Kashmir Gate*, Chippenham 1983.

9   McInsen – I have been unable to find any record of this officer's
services in any of the regimental records. It may have been an
officer on transfer, but I think the simple explanation is that this is
a typing error in Fairweather's memoirs and he is actually referring
to McQueen.

10   John Nicholson died of his wounds on 23 September, 1857,
mourned by the whole Delhi Field Force. Brother Charles survived
the amputation of an arm but never really recovered his health.
After visiting Ireland and America he returned to India with a wife
in 1862 to take up command of a Gurkha regiment. But, on 'the
fifth day of their journey up-country he collapsed and died in a
roadside dak-bungalow, aged 33. He was the fourth and last of the
Nicholson brothers to die in India. Four out of four.' (Allen, *Soldier
Sahibs*, p 330).

11   Wilson – here Fairweather is repeating a famous remark credited to
Nicholson. The man who uttered it was notoriously hot-tempered.
The man he was speaking about was notoriously cautious. Archdale
Wilson was a Norfolkman who had joined the Bengal Artillery in
1819. He had been station commander at Meerut and the Delhi
command was rather thrust upon him. He accepted the authority
despite being in poor health. Holding the Delhi Army together,
waiting to attack until the circumstances seemed right, were
herculean tasks for any man, but especially one recovering from
a severe bout of smallpox. Younger officers counselled for attack
from the early days of the siege. Wilson was wise to wait. If the
Delhi mutineers won it was clear that the British in India would
face a titanic struggle for survival. Victory for the British there,
however, meant doom would surely follow for the mutineers in all

other places. The slurs against Wilson seem to start with impetuous
Nicholson coupled to the genuine dislike of Richard Baird Smith,
a senior engineer. These were taken up by John Lawrence who
had no idea of the problems Wilson was facing at Delhi. A later
critic was Lord Roberts who seems to have been influenced by
the writings of Lawrence's biographer, Bosworth Smith, and H.M.
Vibart, the biographer of Baird Smith. As an example of this I note
that on p 150 (vol ii) of Lawrence's biography, Bosworth Smith
uses a letter of Wilson's to imply he was contemplating retreat but
omits the key words, 'I have determined to hold the position we
now have to the last,'. Sir Henry Norman, Adjutant-General, and a
wise old warrior, later wrote, 'I who was constantly near him never
heard him breathe a word about retiring.' Another contemporary,
Sir George Campbell, wrote that 'sufficient justice has never been
done to Sir Archdale Wilson, who took Delhi. I do believe that
to him individually the success was in a very great measure due.
He was not a showy or a very brilliant man, but he was a good,
cool, solid man' (Campbell, *Memoirs Of My Indian Career*, vol i pp
245–246, London 1893). For a criticism of Wilson – whose victory
led him on to be Lord Clyde's senior artillery officer at Lucknow
– see Vibart, *Richard Baird Smith*, London 1897 and for a spirited
rebuttal of this book and other criticisms see Lee-Warner, *Archdale
Wilson, The Captor Of Delhi*, in the *Fortnightly Review*, 1913.

12   Tyler – an error on Fairweather's part but an understandable one;
he is referring to Mrs Harriet *Tytler*, who was the wife of Captain
Robert Tytler. In her journal she left a brief mention of the
Homfray family with whom she had stayed for a fortnight in 1856.
A baby was born to Harriet during the Siege of Delhi. Christened
Stanley Delhi-Force Tytler, he lived to the ripe age of 91, the
longest living survivor of the event. <u>Further Reading</u>: Sattin, *An
Englishwoman In India*, Oxford 1986.

13   Rotton – the remarkably named Johnny Rotton had been chaplain
at Meerut when the Mutiny broke out. According to Hibbert he
wandered around the Delhi camp in jackboots and a long-sleeved
native choga. He also wrote his own account of the Mutiny. His
family were Anglo-Indian; they included James Rotton, who could
not speak English and the 22 Moslem cousins of Felix Rotton.
According to Dalrymple these young men were 'at that moment
engaged in fighting on the rebel side in Awadh, where they took
an active part in besieging the British Residency in Lucknow'

(Dalrymple, *The Last Mughal*, p 291). <u>Further Reading</u>: Rotton, *The Chaplain's Narrative of the Siege of Delhi*. London 1858.

14 Fairweather seems to be expressing some colour prejudice here, something which seems remarkably rare in his memoirs; young Homfray's family were living in Lucknow in 1856 so it seems likely they were of Anglo-Indian blood.

15 Jones – the Reserve Column at Delhi was commanded by Lt-Colonel John Jones of the 60th Rifles. Their regimental history, hardly surprisingly, says nothing of McQueen's exploit, though it states that the first thing Jones did on entry was to propose and drink a toast to the Queen's health. (Butler, *The Annals Of The King's Royal Rifle Corps Vol III* p 147).

16 Fairweather is right and looting at Delhi was indiscriminate. It was an accepted part of Victorian colonial warfare – up to a point. Usually, as at Delhi, prize agents were appointed by the army to sell the collected plunder. But native troops had different views and usually tried to grab what they could as did many British troops of all ranks. This wholesale theft and destruction of antiquities was not limited to troops. At Delhi the American missionary, William Butler, wandered through the palace and saw in the Jama Masjid the marble slabs said to bear the impress of Mohammed's hand and foot and ' as "looting" was the order of the day, I carried them off...' (quoted in Llewellyn-Jones, p 136).

4

March to Agra – Cawnpore

The Regiment got no rest after Delhi had fallen into our hands, but was ordered at once to join the Column under Greathed[1] which was to follow the retreating sepoys down country. We marched on August 23rd and as we marched through the deserted city across the bridge towards the Jumna, one of the awkward camels, laden with Mess stores, collided against one of the narrow gateways and smashed no end of our precious beer and other liquors, which made us nearly weep as we knew they could not be replaced.

Our first march was to Shadra, just a little way across the river, the second to Ghazi-a-din-huggar (now Gaziabad) and during that march a large number – I forget how many – of our sepoys and camp followers and, sad to say, our Commandant, Captain Wilde, were seized with cholera. Captain Wilde lingered on all night and, in the morning, when the Force marched I was left behind with him in his tent and a large guard, expecting to have to bury him and then follow the Column, but I had got a bottle of champagne from Dr. Clarke of the 2nd Punjab Infantry and the first sip seemed to revive him. He said, 'That is nice. Give me some more'. After a time he so far revived that I ordered him to be taken in a doolie to Delhi.

Just as I put Wilde in his doolie he asked that the remains of the champagne might be placed under his pillow. I thought this a good sign. No doubt feeling utterly weak he asked that half the guard should go back with him to Delhi as the neighbourhood was swarming with fugitive sepoys. He arrived safely. For many weeks he lay in hospital there, almost at death's door, and was not able to rejoin the Regiment until after the Relief of Lucknow. With the other portion of the guard I hastened to catch up the Column and arrived about dinner time.

On going to Mess I was surprised to find three new officers – Captain E. Lane,[1] and Lieutenants Grey[3] and Osborn[4] – who had been attached to the Regiment.

We reached Bulandshahr on September 28th. Here we found a force of rebels occupying a serai[5] and a rebel chief called Walidad Khan in a stronghold close by called Malagarh.[6] The Force advanced on the serai and after battering at the guns it was taken by assault, the 2nd P.I. leading and a stubborn fight they had. While this was going on the 4th Punjab Infantry remained on rearguard with two guns under Major Turner. Some of the rebel cavalry made a detour and attacked our baggage where some sick soldiers were following the Column in doolies. The enemy were driven off before they were able to do much damage, but the brutes murdered several of the Europeans in the doolies. My bearer, who was in the rear of the Column, told me that when the enemy's horsemen were careering along to loot the baggage he had kept them off mine by jabbing at their horses with his spear.

The Force remained at Malagarh for a day and blew up the stronghold of the rebel chief. In doing so, Home, of the Engineers, who had survived the blowing in of the Kashmir Gate, was killed by the explosion.[7] Our next march was to Khoorja where a skeleton was found on the side of the road close to where a Hindu fakir lived. The fakir denied knowing anything about it and he narrowly escaped being hung up, as it was thought impossible but that he must have known something of it, but he appeared to be a wretched half-witted creature. I remember a wild Irishman, Hugh Haly of the Police, getting my bearer's spear, which was stuck up at the door of my tent, and declaring he would like to send it through the fakir and in those days I was afraid he would do so. He afterwards got hold of a screw out of my tent and, seizing the fakir's hand, placed the screw on the back of it and threatened to screw it through unless he confessed to what he knew about the skeleton. He would have done so, I think, had I not told him firmly that I would not allow such a thing in my tent. The skeleton was carefully examined by us doctors and we came to the conclusion that it belonged to a young woman, most probably a European, as it was unlikely that natives would allow one of their own kith and kin to remain exposed like that.

Our next march was to Aligarhi which was occupied by a body of the enemy who decamped on our approach. As the 4th Punjab Infantry advanced to a wicket gate it was suddenly opened and a gun, loaded with pieces of iron, etc., was exploded in our faces. Curiously, no one was hit except a poor bugler who got a piece in the outer corner of his eye. The gun was of a novel description invented by the mutineers from the iron socket of the telegraph posts. These 'telegraph guns' were made from posts which the rebels had dug up and converted into cannon by piercing a touch hole at the small end. These they charged with powder and, on the top of it, nails, stones, fragments of chopped-up wire, etc. We could not account for the number of guns which were said to have been taken by Havelock in each of his engagements and concluded that many of them must have been of this description.

I was puzzled to find that there were no symptoms of injury to the brain in the man who was hit, although it seemed to me that the missile, whatever it was, must have penetrated it. I thought I could feel something hard lying just in front of the ear and above the cheekbone. On cutting down upon this I came across a piece of iron which had apparently been cut off a square rod about three-quarters of an inch square. This poor man, to my amazement, remained apparently well and free from any bad symptoms for two days. I had begun to doubt if my diagnosis of his brain was correct, but I had hardly left the hospital on the second day when I was called back, and before I could reach it he was dead. I have the piece of iron still as a memento of the occasion.

A Company of the 4th Punjab Infantry under Lieutenants Grey and Osborn was left to garrison Aligarh. The Force then went on to Hatras and there an urgent message was received from Agra saying that they were threatened by mutineers from Central India and requesting General Greathed to hurry on with all the speed possible. Orders were therefore issued that the Force should march at five that evening and we marched the livelong night without a halt; so utterly tired and sleepy was I that I determined to fall out of the Column and lie down on the side of the road to get a short sleep. Fastening my horse's bridle round my wrist, I was soon in the Land of Dreams and did not awake until a good part of the baggage animals had passed. I then mounted my horse again and cantered on to try and find the Regiment, but the road was so blocked by baggage animals that I had great difficulty in moving and it was a long time before I caught up with the 4th P.I. at last. I forget the number of miles it is between Hatras and Agra but it was a very weary march and the sun was hot and high when we reached the city. As we filed under the walls of the Fort the ramparts were crowded with the European residents who had taken shelter there and who cheered us as we passed, especially the ladies, waving their handkerchiefs in token of welcome of our arrival. Nearly all the officers commanding regiments of the Column were invited into the Fort to breakfast while we had still to march another mile or two farther on to the parade ground where we were to encamp.

It was 11 o'clock in the day when we arrived there, so that we had really been 18 hours on the march, and everyone was wearied out. As our baggage and tents were far behind McQueen and I lay down on the ground, under the shade of a blanket hung over the pole of a doolie and were soon asleep, but were suddenly roused by some pottering of musketry at the picquets. This soon became a fusillade and McQueen jumped up and got on his horse to gallop to the Picquets, but before he could do so round shot began to bowl through our camp and a body of enemy cavalry charged into it.

In the meantime Captain Paul, commanding, had fallen in the Regiment and formed it into a square. At this moment I perceived that that one of my doolie bearers was lying on the ground with his thigh broken by a round shot, while the rest of the doolie bearers had bolted with their doolies towards some gardens nearby, leaving the poor wretch to be cut up by the sowars. I therefore left the Regiment and running as hard as I could caught hold of the last doolie and brought it back with the bearers by force to where the wounded doolie bearer was lying. I then had the poor man put carefully into the doolie. Suddenly it was apparent I was cut off from the Regiment by the enemy cavalry. The camels and baggage were just arriving in camp and the confusion caused by the round shot among the camels, some of them running about wounded, and one with a leg dangling, along with all the camp followers shouting and screaming with terror, is difficult to describe.

I saw a battery of Horse Artillery as I thought in full flight. It seemed to me that all was lost and therefore the only thing for me to do was retreat with the doolie and wounded bearer to the security of some neighbouring gardens. I then posted myself in a belt of palms to watch the progress of the fight.

For a considerable time the only guns I heard were those of the enemy, with the round shot bowling through the camp like cricket balls; one was bowling along apparently so gently that I thought to put my foot out and stop it, but recollected a story of a man I had heard who had tried this trick and got his leg broken, so I refrained from making the experiment. But at last, to my joy, I heard the sound of our own guns with no corresponding balls coming towards me. Then, one after another, until the whole of our Artillery were playing on the enemy. Gradually I hear their guns sounding less and less frequently until they ceased all together. Before the guns got into action the 9th Lancers, many of them mounted simply in their trousers with their braces hanging down, attacked the enemy's horsemen and very few of them, I believe, left the ground alive. Our frontier cavalry, under Watson,[8] Probyn and Younghusband, were meanwhile watching their opportunity to charge. Watson, the senior, instantly seized on the confusion in the enemy's lines caused by the explosion of a tumbrel and giving the word took their guns in flank and captured the whole line. The enemy then retreated with all haste and were followed by our Force to a distance of 10 miles where, in crossing a small nullah, they had to relinquish the rest of their guns, ammunition and camp equipage. The whole became a prize of the Force.

I tried in vain to reach my Regiment but only met them on return from this successful battle. Everyone was amazed at the utter ignorance of the Agra Garrison as to the enemy's force for they must have actually been encamped within gunshot of us on the morning our arrival. It is said they were just as surprised as we were as they imagined the Force on the encamping ground was only a detachment of troops from the Fort, but when they saw the khaki uniform of the Punjab regiments they cried out to each other 'Delhi Wallah!' and so lost heart.

We were all very proud of this victory on October 10th; not only had we been taken by surprise, but it had been fought while most of the C.Os were not present as they breakfasted in Agra Fort. Great was the rejoicing in the Fort when the news of the victory reached them and they saw the captured cannon being dragged in; one of these pieces was so enormous that it could not pass through any of the gates of the Fort. Our men declared they had captured this gun. We rested here some days and our camp was visited every evening by numbers of ladies and others from the Fort driving out to see their deliverers and inspect the heroes who had first taken Delhi and then marched all those miles to their relief. It was a delightful

The sick and wounded in 'Doolies' within sight of the enemy.

A Dak Gharry, a cross between a stagecoach and a 'perambulating bed', depicted on the Grand Trunk Road.

Starting on the march, an encampment before dawn.

Punjab veterans of the Mutiny. Back row, left to right: Clement Smith, John Coke, Dighton Probyn VC, Henry Daly Charles Batchelor, Clem Brown and Depuis. Front row, left to right: two unknown officers, Herbert Edwardes, George Lawrence, Alfred Wilde and Herbert Clogstown VC.

The bridge of boats at Attock, taken in 1863.

Peshawar Fort seen from a distance.

A contemporary sketch of Home, Salkeld and fellow engineers preparing to blow the Kashmir Gate in Delhi.

The Kashmir Gate, photographed about 1870. The left gateway was the attacking point. It has since been blocked up.

General Sir Colin
Campbell (right)
and his chief-of-staff,
Major-General Sir
William Mansfield.

Punjab Irregular Force sepoys believed to be men of the 4th P.I., *c.*1857.

Hindoo Rao's house, held by the Gurkhas, seen here after the siege.

The Red Fort, Delhi.

Dighton Probyn, VC, a
cavalryman par excellence.

Probyn's great friend, John Watson
VC; both were fearless swordsmen
riding into battle and fighting
mutineers in numerous personal
combats.

A contemporary watercolour of 'Mutinous Sepoys' by George Franklin Atkinson.

John Nicholson, the inspiring leader of the British attacking force who was struck down by a mutineer's bullet and killed during the Storming of Delhi.

John Jones, commanding officer of the 60th Rifles.

John McQueen, a subaltern with the 4th PI, twice recommended for the VC in 1857, who rose to command the Punjab Frontier Force.

Nana Sahib of Bithur, who was responsible for the Cawnpore massacres. He became the British Empire's most wanted man.

The weak British entrenchment at Cawnpore.

Satichaura Gat, a riverside temple where the unarmed British were shot down and hundreds killed.

'The Chamber of Blood': a contemporary sketch of the interior of the building where upwards of 200 women and children were brutally murdered.

The Dulkusha Palace at Lucknow.

The Martiniere College at Lucknow.

Chuttar Manzil Palace at Lucknow.

A Royal Artillery battery sighting a gun at Lucknow, 1857.

Peel and his gunners make a breach during the attack on the Sikanderbagh.

An exterior view of the breach and gateway at Sikanderbagh.

The courtyard at the end of the Sikanderbagh Garden where the mutineers made a last stand. The skeletons scattered on the ground, it is now suggested, were taken out of the building specially for this famous Felice (or Felix) Beato photograph (note the re-excavated doorway at right). The Italian-British photographer Beato was one of the first important war photographers and a pioneer of what would become known as photojournalism.

Willian Martin Cafe VC, 4th PI, hero of the Ruiya debacle.

Colour-Sergeant William Gardiner, 78th Highanders, who won the VC saving the life of his colonel.

change from the perpetual marching we had had and gave us the opportunity of seeing that wonder of the world – the Taj Mahal. McQueen and I rode over one evening to see it. I remember well the effect it had on me when we suddenly came in sight of it at the turn of a road, its white marble cupolas framed in the green of cypress trees, all gilded by the light of an October setting sun – it was a sight which dwells in my memory yet.

At Agra the command of the Force was taken over from Colonel Greathed by Colonel Hope Grant[9] of the 9th Lancers. We then marched to Mynpoorie [Mainpuri] where we expected to meet a force of the enemy but they retired before our arrival. Lieutenant F. Oldfield,[10] who had been one of the refugees at Agra, was now attached to our Regiment. At Mynpoorie, one evening after dinner, when all the others had gone out somewhere, he and I were left alone smoking. He told me he had got the offer of the command of a newly raised police battalion. Before accepting it he had gone to ask the opinion of the brigadier-general and had been persuaded not to leave the 4th Punjab Infantry at present as it was going on further service and it would not look well if he were to leave under such circumstances. He then said that he had a presentiment that the 4th Punjab Infantry would go down to the Relief of Lucknow and that he should be killed there. Of course I laughed at his presentiment and pointed out that it was extremely unlikely that we should go as far as Lucknow. The subject was not alluded to again between us, but in due time we found ourselves at Cawnpore with only a slight skirmish at Kanouj on the way.

Our first objective on reaching Cawnpore was to visit the Slaughter House where the women and children saved from the Massacre at the boats were first confined and, on the approach of Havelock,[11] ordered to be murdered by the arch fiend, Nana Sahib.[12] The place where this deed of horror was perpetrated was a building used as a dispensary. It was built in the form of a quadrangle enclosing an open square, in the centre of which stood a tree, in the trunk of which were numerous cuts as from a sword. From one of these I

Hope Grant, superb cavalry commander of HM 9th Lancers.

was told one of Havelock's men had taken a lock of golden hair and kept it as a memento. This tree was afterwards cut down and made into small memorial crosses like the wooden one that was at first placed over the well where the murdered ones were thrown. They were sold for a rupee each to aid a memorial to be got up of and the Massacre and I was able to get one.

Inside the dispensary building the evidence of the massacre was everywhere. There were pieces of mattress lying here and there soaked in blood and the walls in many places was smeared with it. In some places there were marks as if bloody hands had been wiped on the walls. I saw fragments of women's clothes lying about, a pair of stays in one place, a lady's hat and one or two children's shoes. The well where all the bodies were thrown by the murderers was filled up when I visited it, but the marks on the ground were still visible where they had dragged the bodies to the well. It is impossible to describe the bitterness of feeling and the craving for revenge that possessed us while we surveyed all these horrors. We never said a word to each other, or made a remark as we passed through, but our teeth were clenched and we inwardly swore that we would have vengeance on the demons who did this deed. We afterwards visited General Wheeler's entrenchment; it was no entrenchment at all but only a barrack with no defences whatever. It was all battered with shot and the wall showed signs of the deadly effect of the fire.[13]

We only remained here a short time and were sent across the Ganges to guard the bridge of boats. Here we stayed for some time until all the supplies for the Garrison at Lucknow had been brought safely across the river. It was here that Captain C. Lane left us for the Commissariat and Lieutenant Willoughby[14] of a Balooch Regiment in Bombay joined us.

A wing of the 93rd, 64th and 5th Fusliers who had gone up country also joined us here as well as a company of Royal Artillery. I can't tell you what effect the sound of the bagpipes had upon me when the Highlanders began to approach across the bridge of boats. It thrilled me like electricity and for a moment I could but not fancy I was in India but far away upon some brown hillside in Auld Scotland. The whole camp turned out to see the 93rd as they passed and as they heaved along with their tartans and plumes many exclaimed, 'These are the boys to do it!' I could not help comparing their strong appearance and fresh ruddy complexions with the poor, worn-out, pale-faced and dusty regiments in their dirty khaki uniform which had borne the brunt of the Siege of Delhi and the long march from that to Cawnpore.

Notes

1 Greathed – this was Colonel Edward Greathed commanding H.M. 8th Foot.
2 Lane – possibly a small typing error here in Fairweather's manuscript; this was Lt. C. Lane formerly of the 26th Bengal Native Infantry.
3 Grey – he had been transferred from the 16th B.N.I. which had seemed disaffected and, along with the 26th B.N.I., been disarmed at Mian Mir on 13 May 1857.
4 Osborn – R. D. Osborn was, like Lane, formerly an officer of the 26th B.N.I.
5 Serai – a native inn.
6 Malagarh – in his journal for 1 October 1857, Engineer officer Lt. Arthur Moffatt Lang wrote: 'Here I am seated in the cool open room over the river gateway of the stronghold of that scoundrel Walidad Khan … This is our third day here and our occupation is the demolition of this Fort; we live very well on plunder, on the geese, ducks and pigeons of Walidad, from whose stores we are also well provided with tables and chair, plates and dishes; beautiful beer, unlimited in quantity; cones on cones of lump sugar, and numberless great yellow bottles of rose water with which we bathe! In fact we are living in style, conquerors and marauders … How delighted I felt when I saw the Fort and knew it was deserted and that we had not to take it. Our light guns would have been of no avail against the high, thick, earthen ramparts. It has a very strong profile indeed, this Maligarh. It is rectangular with round bastions (still higher than the ramparts) and has three gateways all round – no end of corners. I should say it *had*, for we have levelled

a long line of rampart, burned one gateway, and blown in another.'
(Blomfield p 106).

7   Home was killed setting the last mine in the ditch below the walls
of the fort. Lt. Lang rushed over and found his friend's body in the
hollow of a well, 'all mangled and covered with dust: poor fellow
his legs were broken in two places, his arms broken and one nearly
torn off; his death must have been instantaneous.' (Blomfield p 107).
His gravestone can still be seen in Bulandshahr Anglican Cemetery.

8   Watson – born in 1829, John enlisted in the Bombay Army in 1848
and, on transfer to the Bombay Fusiliers served with them in the
2nd Sikh War. His courage was soon noticed, especially the way
in which he carried the regimental colour up to the breach at the
storming of Multan. He seems to have been discontented with his
regiments because he transferred twice again before deciding to
become a cavalryman. Fairweather makes reference to Watson's role
as firstly adjutant, and then commander, of the 1st Punjab Cavalry.
Along with Probyn of the 2nd P.C. and George Younghusband of
the 5th P.C. the trio were in the thick of battles during the Mutiny.
This resulted at Lucknow in both Watson and Probyn winning
the Victoria Cross in the same action. During the Mutiny young
Watson was wounded three times. Shortly after this he was asked
to raise a regiment of Sikh cavalry. It was called at first the 4th
Sikh Cavalry but soon became famous as the 13th Bengal Lancers
(Watson's Horse). During the 2nd Afghan War Watson served with
the Kurram Field Force. It was his last campaign. John Watson died
in 1919 aged 89 years. Writing of Probyn and Watson's years with
the Punjab Irregular Force the latter's son said: 'It is impossible
not to mention these two happy warriors together. They were
devoted and lifelong friends. I have heard each say of the other that
the Almighty could not find too good a place for him. Yet they
differed much, in style as well as in appearance. Probyn tall, dark,
bearded, exceedingly handsome, was the living embodiment of the
pomp and circumstance of war. Watson, fair-haired, blue-eyed, very
powerful and of medium stature, cared less for appearances than
for practical efficiency. Both were superb horsemen; but Watson
rose in his stirrups instead of bumping the saddle in the fashion
of English cavalry, even on ceremonial parades. Probyn called this
'jogging along like an old farmer.' Both were great swordsmen; and
here they were alike, for they both used a curved sword and 'hit
first and hit hardest' was their only rule. And they were alike in a

simple faith, which they were not too bashful to express. To read family prayers, to go to Church at least once every Sunday, and to sing hymns in the drawing-room after tea was their constant habit. It sounds a little strange in the twentieth century, but in Victorian days there were many like them.' (Watson, pp 124–125).

9   Grant – the rising star on the military scene, following his superb handling of the 9th Lancers in the Mutiny, James Hope Grant was born in Perthshire in 1808, joining the 9th Lancers when he was eighteen. He saw action with them in the 1st Anglo-Chinese War 1839–42, both Sikh Wars and the Sind Campaign before the glory days of 1857–58. This led him to be made a general and on to the command of British forces in the 2nd Anglo-Chinese War 1859–60. He died full of honours in 1875. Tall, rather gaunt and spare, Grant was an expert horsemen and tough soldier who read little except the Bible. It was said that he owed his appointment as brigade-major to Lord Saltoun in the first China campaign because of his skill on the violincello so that the commander had a colleague for musical duets! Further Reading: Knollys, *Life Of General Sir Hope Grant*, Edinburgh 1894.

10 Oldfield – according to the regimental history, he transferred from the 9th B.N.I. on 6 November 1857. His previous regiment had detachments at Etawah, Bulandshahr and Mynpoorie and mutinied in all three stations but, almost uniquely, it was a bloodless revolt and the men basically went off to Delhi ignoring their British officers. More than 30 years later one of them was quoted as saying: 'But, Sahib, the 9th Regiment was almost the only regiment which did not murder its officers. We gave each of them three months pay in advance from the Treasury. And escorted them, and their families within a safe distance of Agra before went went to Delhi, and all of us who lived through the Mutiny were pardoned by the Government.' (Gimlette p 95).

11 Havelock – along with Nicholson, Henry Havelock was the main Victorian hero of the Mutiny and is, certainly, the British Army's greatest example of a man of God as a warrior. Born in 1795, the son of a rich Sunderland shipbuilder, he had not wanted to become a soldier but a lawyer. An argument with his father, who refused him certain expenses, made Henry decide to follow an elder brother into the Army. Deciding to serve in India he diligently mastered Persian and Hindustani before setting sail for the East. He always tried to be a 'Christian soldier' and his troops in the 1st

Anglo-Burmese War became known as 'Havelock's Saints'. His marriage in 1829 to the daughter of a leading Baptist missionary only encouraged his belief that prayer meetings, sermons and Bible lessons were good for the common soldiers under his command. Promotion came slowly – it took Havelock 23 years just to get to captain, but his brilliance in the 1st Afghan and Gwalior Wars saw him jump, without purchase, to the rank of lieutenant-colonel. In 1856 he commanded a division in the Persian War. Arriving back in India he was seen by all as something of a saviour and immediately given command of the Cawnpore Relief Force. His army moved with extreme ruthlessness though, to be fair to Havelock, he tried to prevent several of the excesses of officers under his command; he arrived too late at Cawnpore to avert a terrible disaster, then went on to Lucknow in what is usually termed its 'first relief', but was in fact a reinforcement of the besieged garrison. His death there on 24 November was poignant; he died smiling and in his son's arms with the words, 'See how a Christian can die.' One of Havelock's artillery officers described him thus: 'His figure was slight and small, but neat and erect. He was always well-mounted, and a good rider, quick of speech, too, and ready of retort, grandiloquent and Napoleonic in his style both in writing and in conversation. He knew infantry and brigade movements thoroughly well. Everybody knows that he was God-fearing and blameless in his life, yet he was sterner and more severe than seems to be generally understood. His face was older than his years, and much tanned by the Indian sun; his moustache, whiskers and beard being rather long and perfectly white.' (Maude, *Memories Of The Mutiny,* vol i, pp 39–40).

12 Sahib – the greatest villain of British imperial history, Nana Sahib was the adopted son of the last Peshwa, leader of the proud Mahrattas, who surrendered to the British in 1818. Nana, whose real name was Dhondo Pant, was a man with a grievance; his 'father' had made him his sole heir but, on the latter's death in 1851, the H.E.I.C. refused to grant him the vast pension enjoyed by the Peshwa. Nana Sahib even sent an English-speaking, cultured young man named Azimullah Khan to London to plead his case but all to no avail. On the outbreak of the Mutiny he wavered for a time in supporting the rebels. It has been suggested by some historians, notably Ward, that Azimullah sneakily encouraged his master to declare against the foreigners. Following the massacres he fled and became for half a century the Raj's Public Enemy Number

1. He was never brought to justice and it is now thought that he probably died in the jungles of Nepal within a year or so of the Mutiny's end. <u>Further Reading</u>: Gupta, *Nana Sahib And The Rising At Cawnpore*, Oxford 1963.

13 The horrors of the Slaughter House and Well at Cawnpore are simply and vividly told by Fairweather. His determination to revenge this deed was shared by all who saw the spot and many who just heard of the atrocity. More than 200 women and children had been bloodily slaughtered, then thrown, in some cases still alive, into a deep well. Later, after the Mutiny, the site was cleared and turned into a park, the most sacred spot in British India, where wheels of carriages had to be muffled out of respect. The site of the well is now capped with concrete and the park has become a happy playground for youngsters. Nana Sahib is now considered a hero by many Indians and a bust of him stands close by the grave of those who, if he did not actually agree to murder, he did nothing to save. <u>Further Reading</u>: the definitive account of the Cawnpore Massacres is Ward, *Our Bones Are Scattered*, London 1996; for a succinct and balanced retelling, though it tries to downplay the horror of the event almost too much, read Mukherjee, *Spectre Of Violence*, New Delhi 1998.

14 Willoughby – Edward Cotgrave Parr Willoughby had served in the Crimean War and Persian War; he transferred to the 4th P.I. on 7 November 1857 from the 19th Bombay Infantry. He was a brother of George Willoughby, one of the nine who had blown up the Magazine in Delhi at the start of the siege.

5

Storming of Lucknow – Sikanderbagh – Relief of the Garrison

From October 31st we marched 14 miles towards Lucknow and passed several places where Havelock had had to fight his way. In some places barricades had been thrown across the road and places for guns to sweep the road as people approached. At another place there was a long bazaar lining the road for a quarter of a mile, with a narrow gate at each end, and every house loopholed for musketry. On the entrance gate we found a soda water bottle on the top of a stick, no doubt placed there by one of Havelock's soldiers as evidence of their victory.

We were now in Oudh which had been so recently annexed and which gave evidence of its hostility to us in the deserted condition of every village. About mid-day word was brought that a lot of armed men had been observed in a village we had passed, so a Company of our Regiment, with one of the 93rd Highlanders and some cavalry and guns were sent back to drive them out and, though they nearly all cleared out before our arrival, some 12 or 20 of them were killed, several of whom were sepoys. The only casualty on the occasion was

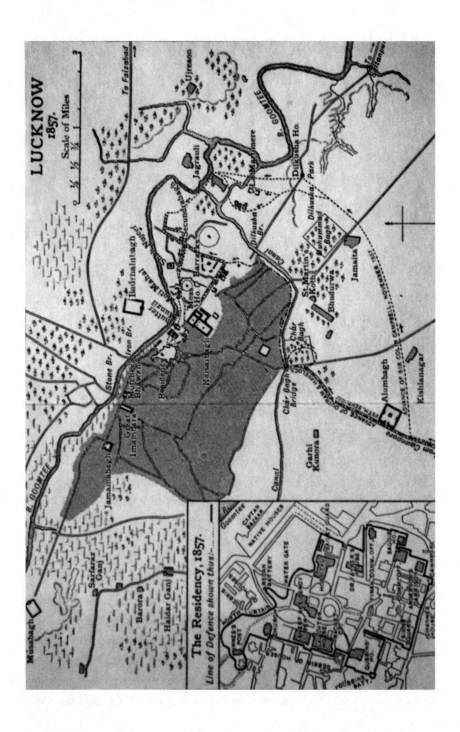

one of our men, a Sikh, who was shot dead upon entering one of the houses, but his assailant paid the penalty with his life.

On November 1st we marched 15 miles and passed two other places where Havelock had had to fight his way. One of them was a small stream where they had broken down the bridge, with a loopholed village on the other side; this was the first bridge we had come upon broken down, which seemed extraordinary seeing it was such an effectual way to impede our progress. Our men were awfully amused with the Highlanders on the march. They could not make out what they were at all, and kept examining them all over from head to foot, always ending in a loud fit of laughter. They seemed, however, to get on capitally together, for I saw one or two of the Highlanders walking along between a number of Pathans, keeping up apparently an animated conversation with them, the one party talking in the broadest Scotch and the other the most guttural Pushtoo.

As we neared our camping ground the boom of the cannon from Lucknow became very distinct. How eager it made us to rush on; there is something peculiarly delightful in the idea of going to the relief of a beleaguered place, quite different from going to the assault of an enemy stronghold. The name of our halting ground was the Bunnee Bridge which was within 14 miles of Lucknow. Here we were ordered to remain for the present. But on the same evening we were told to be ready to march the next morning at 4 o'clock; during the night the Brigadier got intelligence of a body of the enemy who were lurking about in the villages on our flanks ready to fall on the baggage when we had passed, so we did not march till 7 o'clock.

We had scarcely gone a mile when firing was heard ahead and we found our advance guard pretty briskly engaged with a party of the enemy who had established themselves in a village through which the road passed. Just as we began to come up a clear hearty cheer told us the place was won. The country here was covered with villages of this kind and as we found each of them filled with sepoys and armed men we were under the necessity of zigzagging about from one to the other, taking and burning them. Every field too had some of them lying hid in the tall crops and waiting for an opportunity to attack the baggage. At one time a whole line of their cavalry and infantry appeared drawn up in front of us. We fully expected them to give battle but as we advanced upon them the skunks as usual vanished upon our approach.

We were kept at this work till about 2 o'clock when we returned to camp fairly tired out for we had to go at the double for a great part of the way. Two of the Highlanders were killed, but our loss otherwise was small, only 20 altogether from all regiments being wounded. The loss of our Regiment was 5 wounded. I was delighted with the quiet way the Highlanders went through their work, no excitement and no worry, but whatever they had to do when they were under a heavy fire was done as coolly and apparently with as much indifference as if they had been doing their everyday work. Our men were much amused with a bugle boy of theirs; every time he sounded a call, which he always did with immense energy, they fairly threw back their heads and laughed with astonishment at the air with which he did it and the swagger with which he strutted off afterwards.

The admiration of our men for the Highlanders was immense and the music of the bagpipes delighted them, especially the Pathans of the Regiment who have an instrument very like the chanter of a bagpipe, the sound of which often reminded me of the pipes. I cannot say how many of the enemy were killed on this day for they were shot down in villages, tops of trees and rank fields of Indian corn and sugar cane. McQueen, with 100 of our fellows slew about 26 of them in one village and helped bayonet about 13 more in another. Altogether I should say 150 to 200 had been killed, a great number of whom were very mutinous sepoys and the rest armed villagers. Oudh you must know was the most warlike country in Hindustan and it was from this that most of our old sepoys came. We also took two field pieces and it is said that when the Highlanders charged and took these a European¹ was actually laying one of them to fire on us. Of course he was shot on the spot. I forget if I mentioned that a similar case occurred at Delhi and that I saw him when brought in as a prisoner. He was executed next day.

After finishing our work we encamped. On the evening of November 4th an order reached us late at night that we were to form part of a convoy next day to escort stores etc., to Alum Bagh, a post held by our troops three miles from Lucknow. The rest of the Force consisted of a wing of the 93rd, portions of the 5th and 53rd Foot, a battery of six field pieces, a squadron of the 9th Lancers and some Punjab Cavalry. We thought it very curious that whenever any work was to be done our Regiment was always selected for the purpose instead of the 2nd Punjab Infantry, which was the senior regiment and our men, though proud of it, thought they got more than their share of hard knocks. We were prepared when we started to have to fight our way there and back and made arrangements accordingly taking no tents and only a supply of food for three days in case of necessity. The Force which stayed behind in camp were also prepared the whole day to come out to our assistance in case of hearing the sound of a heavy attack on us.

We were agreeably surprised, however, when not an enemy appeared the whole way into Alum Bagh where we landed the stores with safety, to the great delight of the small garrison there who had been rather hard up for supplies for some days back. They had been so closely beleaguered as to have been unable even to obtain grass for their cattle and horses. As soon as they heard of our arrival out rushed all the grass-cutters, who were busy the whole day carrying in bundles, so they had a good supply before we left. Some elephants who had been half-starved for days were let loose in a field of sugar cane and the way they handled their trunks was something wonderful – armful after armful of the cane disappearing as if by magic.

As the last of the baggage was passing into Alum Bagh a large number of the enemy, principally cavalry, began to hover among the trees on the side of the road as if to attack us. So our Regiment and a company or two of Highlanders went out to drive them off, which they did very sharply, the sneaks as usual not being able to stand a minute.

They once gathered pretty thickly at one spot and formed into line as if to charge us, but a couple of our field pieces were sent forward at them and one or two shells went crashing into their ranks and soon made them take leg bail, followed by our cavalry and guns. Some time after this I was lying down in a tope of trees taking a nap with the reserve company of the Highlanders, who were also mostly asleep, when there was a sudden call, 'Fall in, fall in, my men'. When I jumped up to see what was happening I saw our guns and cavalry coming tearing through the trees as hard as they could lick and we were expecting every second to see the enemy hard on their heels but no enemy appeared; as they came scampering towards us we could see each man with his handkerchief flapping about his ears as hard as ever he could, while now and then a peal of laughter would be heard. The whole cause of this disgraceful retreat, as we afterwards discovered, was a nest of hornets. They had accidentally been disturbed and in their attack on both men and horses driven them off the field. On our return journey we had a large number of sick and wounded at the Alum Bagh to escort back and our Regiment, with a company of the 93rd and some cavalry were on rearguard as it was thought most likely that the enemy would try to annoy us. But not a man came near us and we arrived safely in camp about 10 o'clock much to the astonishment of the people there who fancied we would not be back for days.

We remained at our old camping ground until the morning of the 12th when we marched to Alum Bagh. Here we encamped, our Force having been considerably increased from the previous day by drafts of the 93rd, 53rd and other regiments and also by 150 men of the Naval Brigade with several 24–pounder guns. It did one's heart good to see the jolly old English tars again and it gave the sepoys an idea of our power and resources seeing the many different kinds of soldiers we could bring into the field.

On November 13th the whole Force was paraded for the inspection of Sir Colin Campbell[2] who had joined us a few days previously. On the following morning (14th) we commenced our march for the relief of the garrison. Before starting Sir Colin marched along our line addressing a few words to each Regiment as he passed. He had hardly passed the 4th Punjab Infantry when a sepoy suddenly fell down in the ranks and, grovelling on the ground, said he had such a pain in his interior that he couldn't march. I was furious with the man for I was convinced that it was merely a pretence and I was ashamed of this public exhibition. In my hurried examination of him I ordered that he be taken to hospital and I was much surprised and grieved to hear afterwards that he had died there.

On the march we were in the advance with the 93rd Highlanders. We did not like the route that Havelock had taken but made a flanking movement to the right round the city so as to avoid street fighting as much as possible and from which Havelock's column had suffered severely. We saw little of the enemy till about 1 o'clock, for though they swarmed in the fields and gardens a round shot or two soon dispersed them. About that time, however, they showed some determination to dispute our further progress by bringing two heavy guns to play on us and lined the tops of the trees etc. with their sharpshooters. It was not without some difficulty that they were cleared out of the woods and gardens and the 93rd lost a good many men in capturing the two guns. The sailors of the Naval Brigade seemed highly delighted with the wild screams and cheers of our men as they dashed out of the trees after the retreating Pandis and took off their caps shouting 'Bravo!' as we passed.

This was a nasty kind of fighting for the regiments were so divided and lost to each other among the fields and woods that we ran a great risk of being hit by our own men. After this we went on a little further to a large enclosure in which the late King of Oudh had a country house called Dilkusha Bagh – or 'garden of the heart's delight'. Here we intended to encamp for the night, but we had scarcely rested half an hour when the dropping fire of our picquets in front got hotter and hotter, and at last two guns began to send their shot unpleasantly near us. A canister shot came close to us, breaking a camel's leg, while a round shot went slap into a company of Highlanders who were lying down, killing 3 and wounding 2 of them. This could not be submitted to any longer, so our Regiment, with some others, was sent forward to clear the garden. There was a deal of warm skirmishing for a while. They were our matches at that. So Paul sounded the double and away went our fellows helter skelter, shouting, cheering and firing as fast as they could. Pandi could not stand this but scuttled while our fellows chased them clean out of the wood and followed them up to a small village beyond. Here our men did not stop, but leaped over the walls after them, shoving their rifles through the very loopholes made by the Pandis for their own use. The villains were flabbergasted and made no resistance, but chucking down their arms, fled as fast as their legs would carry them, but not before some 30 of them were bayoneted.

The Regiment got great credit for the spirited way in which they did this piece of service and Sir Colin Campbell gave us the post of danger we had taken to keep. This was not a very pleasant duty, however, for it was far in advance of the rest of the Force and we were obliged to be the whole night on the cold earth (and cold enough it was too), almost without covering and every minute expecting to be attacked by the enemy. I may mention here to show how faithful our servants were during the Mutiny that my khitmatgar crawled down in the dark to where we were with some cold meat and bread which was very acceptable. We had little disturbance from the enemy during the night, except for one or two of them who sneaked quietly up in the dark and fired a few shots in our direction, but at daylight they seemed to discover that we were unsupported and began to press us a good deal, again taking possession of the village from which we had driven them and which we had abandoned, keeping an incessant crossfire on us. Had we not got a kind of pit or depression in the ground which gave us some shelter we should have lost a lot of men but, though they kept threatening to attack us the whole day and kept an incessant shower of bullets playing over us, we had only one man hit.

At night we were rather disgusted to find we were not to be relieved, but were to have another night of it and, as it was known that we were to go into Lucknow next day, our fellows were highly indignant at the idea of their being left here to bring up the rear. Next morning we were astonished to find that the 2nd Punjab Infantry was sent down to relieve us while we went back to camp to form part of the leading column that was to go into Lucknow.

When we reached camp we snatched a hasty breakfast consisting of chunks of cold meat, without bread, washed down by strong draughts of tea without sugar or milk. Some men endeavoured to wash and dress but that was a difficult proceeding under the circumstances.

The column was soon in motion and we fell into our places behind the 93rd Highlanders. When we began to get under fire Lieutenant Oldfield, who had told me at Mynpoorie of his presentiment of being killed at Lucknow, and who had never spoken to me about it, although he had been on one or more occasions on duties where he stood a good chance of being killed, now drew up his horse beside me and reminded me of the circumstance. I made a poor endeavour to take his mind off the subject, but he went on to tell me that he didn't wish the horse he was riding to be sold, but to be given to his brother. His sword, revolver and watch he wished to be sent to his father. He said I would find in his writing-desk a number of letters addressed which he asked me to post, which, of course, I promised to do, but told him to try and get rid of these morbid feelings.

There was a good deal of skirmishing as we skirted the suburbs. It was only when we had advanced along several streets that the full storm of musketry was opened on us. It was certainly appalling for a time and everyone cowered behind what shelter they could get. Again we advanced and found that the hottest fire proceeded from a large enclosed garden surrounded by a strong loopholed wall, 20 feet high, with bastions at the corners. As we defiled up a narrow lane which ran parallel with the long wall of the garden, some 40 or 50 yards from it, we were exposed to the full force of the firing from within. There would have been many more casualties here had we not been protected by a wall that ran along the right side of the road. At one point there was an opening in this wall, where a road passed through towards the garden, and across this exposed place everyone made a rush as they came up to it. A poor syce had been shot dead while crossing it and I had to jump over his body as I ran. When we got to the end of the wall we were told to lie down under its shelter till Peel's guns[4] had effected a breach in the nearest bastion. Thus we all got mixed up with the Highlanders. I heard Colonel Leith-Hay,[5] who commanded the 93rd at this time and who had been at the assault of Sebastopol,[6] say that he had never been under such a fierce fire as we were then lying under. It took a considerable time before the guns made any impression on the strong wall, but at last a breach was made and Sir Colin Campbell, who was present, called upon the troops to storm.

As will usually happen when men get mixed up behind a shelter there was just a slight hesitation for a second. Our Subedar-Major, Gokul Singh, a Dogra, stepped out into the open and waving his tulwar over his head called to our men to come on. Paul at the same time gave the order to sound the advance at the double. Our men with a wild cheer rushed towards the breach at the same time as the Highlanders. Some say even before them. So pleased was Sir Colin with the gallant action of Subedar-Major[7] Gokul Singh[8] that he at once asked his name, took a note of it, and brought it to the attention of the Governor-General, who publicly thanked him by name in General Orders (undated).

While part of our men were forcing their way along the narrow breach with the Highlanders, another party, led by young Willoughby, made their way round to the front entrance of the place. This was defended by an entrenchment and two small brass guns. Our men's blood was up and they carried everything before them. The enemy at once retired within the gates and tried to shut them but Subedar

Muckurab Khan[9] thrust his left arm with the shield upon it between the leaves of the gate and so prevented its closing. It was forced open by those who followed him and on entering the garden they were met by those who had entered by the breach.

After our men were fairly inside, the work of death commenced; Sikhs and Highlanders vied with each other in ferocity. There were two lofty towers, one at each side of the gate, with a spiral staircase in each. Up these some of the enemy had taken shelter and were keeping up a fire on our men below. So these as well as the bastions had first to be cleared of the enemy. This was no easy matter as only one man could ascend the stairs at a time and a single man at the top could thus defend against all-comers. At last, however, the difficulty was overcome and all who had taken refuge in these places were shot or bayoneted. In the meantime others of the storming party gradually drove the rebels back through the bushes until they got possession of a small house in the middle of the garden. The farther end of the garden was closed by a long double-storied building with verandahs both below and above. This stretched nearly from wall to wall of the garden, leaving only a space on either side for doors opening into an enclosure behind, with a semi-circular wall of the same height as the rest of the garden wall. Into this building and enclosure the rebels were gradually driven while our men took up their position in the small house in the centre of the garden half-hidden by trees and bushes; from there a prolonged fire of musketry was kept up between it and the building where the enemy had con-gregated at the end of the garden.

Many casualties occurred here among our men. Captain Lumsden,[10] interpreter to the 93rd, was killed at some distance to the right of the central house. McQueen noticed that the body was in danger of being burned by some rubbish which had taken fire near it. To prevent this he ran out and, while he stooped to drag the body away, he felt as if someone had given him a severe kick behind. He turned in a rage to see who it was, at the same time mechani-cally clapping his hand to the part and, seeing no one, looked at his hand and found it covered with blood. This wound was to keep him in hospital for about five months as the bullet could never be discovered and remains in him to this day.

While all this was going on the bastions and other places on the walls and the houses round the garden were being cleared of the enemy until a final assault was made on their final position at the far end of the garden. They had barricaded the door on the left of the double-storied house but our men forced their way through the one on the right and the carnage began. The enemy, hampered by their numbers, crowded away to the corner behind the left hand door. There they were all shot and bayoneted to the last until all lay – the living and the dead – piled up to the height of my breast. I saw the body of a woman lying with a cross-belt upon her, and by her side a dead baby also shot with two bullet wounds in it (through the child's thigh), the poor mother had tied it round with a rag. Such a thing sounds terrible, but it must be remembered that the woman had evidently been fighting against us and in such a mortal conflict, when men are nearly mad with excitement, they hardly know what they are doing.

McQueen told me he had seen a Highlander bayonet another woman and, on his upbraiding him for such a brutal act, he said he turned upon him like a madman, and for a minute he almost expected to be run through with his bayonet; the very next moment a bullet sent the man to Kingdom Come.

This enclosure, called Secundra Bagh,[11] was garrisoned by 2,000 of the enemy, all of whom lay slaughtered there with the exception of one man who escaped over the wall to tell ghastly tales. Our loss in the garden was very severe – the 93rd Highlanders alone lost nearly a company of their men and our poor Regiment lost 72 killed and wounded, including 3 out of the 4 officers who had gone into action. Lieutenant Oldfield was shot pretty early in the day near the elbow and severing the large artery in that neighbourhood. The Assistant-Surgeon of the Highlanders put a tourniquet on it to stop the bleeding and he was brought to me where I had established my hospital just outside the wall. I wished then and there to undo the tourniquet and tie the artery, but Oldfield implored me to leave him alone as he said he had lost so much blood already that he would surely die if he lost any more. However, I couldn't allow the tourniquet to remain for fear of strangling the arm and I therefore cautiously opened it. There was a little spurt of blood from the artery and poor Oldfield fainted away. All I could do then was merely bandage all his fingers and the arm up to the wound so as to prevent strangulation and carefully re-apply the tourniquet, hoping that I would get more time and assistance to do an operation by and by.

Poor Paul was blown up in an explosion of gunpowder in one of the bastions, along with 2 native officers and 2 men, and was terribly burnt before his wadded coat (meerzai) could be torn off him. Young Willoughby, who had only joined us shortly before, alone escaped unharmed.

Towards evening the roar of battle, the crashing of musketry all round, the cannon shot from the Kaiser Bagh crashing through the trees overhead and cutting down branches etc., was indescribable. I had got all my wounded comfortably laid in a sheltered spot close to the wall of the garden with one rezai[12] under them and another over. These I had seized from the Commissariat despite the objection of the officer-in-charge who said they were only meant for Europeans. I told him I would give a receipt but refused to give them up. At this moment, however, a rumour suddenly came out that the Secundra Bagh was going to blow up. Immediately a panic seized the doolie bearers and they bolted with their doolies carrying off Paul, McQueen and Oldfield. After diligent research Paul and McQueen were at last discovered, but poor Oldfield's whereabouts were a mystery till next morning when the doolie bearers again brought him to my hospital. I was very anxious to find out how his arm looked after being all night with a tourniquet round it. When I removed the bandages I was somewhat suspicious of its colour though I hoped it would be all right. With the aid of Dr Clark,[13] 2nd

Punjab Infantry, I then removed the tourniquet, tied the artery, then carefully re-bandaged it and hoped all would be well. In fact I rallied Oldfield with his presentiment of being killed at Lucknow and, as the wounded were being sent back to the Dilkusha, I sent off all three wounded officers with a bottle of beef tea under each of their pillows and some biscuits.

Along with Paul a very fine old Sikh Subedar named Summa Singh, and one of the smartest N.C.Os of the Regiment, whose name I have forgotten, were also badly scorched and sent back with the rest of the wounded. The scene in the garden on the morning after the fight was terrible but at the same time gave one a feeling of gratified revenge. Bodies were lying thickly strewn amongst the trees and bushes, while in some places, where they had made a stand, the bodies of the enemy lay three or four deep. But the most dreadful slaughter was in the small enclosure at the far end of the garden to which all had retreated. Here the corpses were lying piled in some places as high as my waist. The carnage here had been frightful. The walls were covered with bullet marks and the bodies showed that the bayonets of the Highlanders and tulwars of the Sikhs and Pathans had finished the work, (I also noticed the bodies of several women among the slain and one it was said had on a pouch belt and had been fighting like a man). You may think me a savage but I tell you I gloated over the sights of this charnel house and who did not who saw the Slaughter House at Cawnpore? It was the only feeling of satisfied vengeance we had yet had. It gave the more satisfaction to know by the buttons on their coats that these were the very fiends who had committed the atrocities at Cawnpore.

On this day (November 16th), several more of the strongholds between us and the Residency were taken. The garrison there also made a sortie and unmasked some batteries the mutineers had been quietly erecting for the occasion. The enemy were driven from all points and a junction was formed with the garrison. Tremendous was the cheering when this took place. It was taken up and passed along by the detached bodies of troops all over the place till the whole country seemed to resound with hurrahs. Sir Colin rode in that same night and dined with Outram in the Residency, the toast of the evening being the Sikhs and the Highlanders.

The 4th Punjab Infantry were left to garrison the Secundra Bagh. The Force remained about 9 or 10 days while the garrison, with the women and children, guns and stores and everything that could be brought away were, by degrees, quietly removed and sent back on the road to Cawnpore. During these days a steady stream of members of the garrison came filing past the Secundra Bagh, many of them poor ladies dressed in black, who had lost their husbands and other relatives. Many of these we asked to come in and have some refreshment as they passed. It was worth anything to see the way they enjoyed the long untasted delicacies. The first thing they nearly all asked for was bread and butter while the men gloried in a glass of beer.

A few days after I had sent away my wounded a messenger came from Oldfield, who was in hospital at the Dilkusha, imploring me to come and see him as he was very ill. I got on my horse and without any escort rode back the way we came to the Dilkusha. There, as I dreaded, I found mortification had not only begun in Oldfield's arm but had spread to his side so that nothing could be done for the poor fellow. I sat up with him all night listening to his instructions and a dreary night it was in a room filled with wounded and dying men. In the morning Oldfield passed away and I buried him in a corner of the ground at Dilkusha, beside poor Paul who, I heard, had died in his doolie while being conveyed to the Dilkusha. Poor old Summa Singh and the N.C.O. I mentioned, as well as many more who had been blown up, died here from their injuries.

I then rode back to the Regiment in the Secundra Bagh. Here I found that two of the officers from the Residency, Captain O. Smith,[14] who had been adjutant of the mutinied 48th Native Infantry, and Lieutenant O'Dowda[15] had been attached to us. At length the last of the Lucknow garrison had been removed to the Dilkusha and the evacuation by the relieving force began. The whole Force had been lying on extended picquet duty these operations. During the night of November 22nd the troops in the Residency, and those holding positions in the neighbourhood, all quietly retired inwards through the picquets, the guns having been previously sent on ahead.

The 4th Punjab Infantry formed the rearguard and was the last to retire. Sir Colin Campbell came and lay down with the Regiment in extended order waiting until everything had gone well ahead. At one time there was an alarm as if the enemy had discovered we were retreating and there was a great deal of musketry firing in the direction of the Kaiser Bagh. Since all the guns had been retired Sir Colin recalled a rocket battery and sent a few rockets to show we were still there and on the alert. After a short time the firing nearly ceased. Then, about midnight, we fell in and followed the retreating army. In the dark we had difficulty in finding the road back to Dilkusha and I, thinking I knew the road from having ridden back to see Oldfield, took it upon me to guide the Regiment. Before long we knew, by the pottering of musketry on our right that we were getting too near the city, but eventually we reached the Dilkusha all right. It was said that a man had gone to sleep in the Residency on the night of the retirement and only awoke in the morning to find the place deserted. You can imagine his astonishment but he managed to escape without being pursued.

We remained at the Dilkusha one day during which the only annoyance the enemy gave us was sending a few round shot into our camp from a great distance. To show the difficulty that I had with the conveyance of my wounded men let me say I had no more than six doolies and a few camels with 'kajowars'.[16] I was obliged to place many of my wounded upon the top of baggage carts and some even on ammunition wagons sitting on shot and shell.

Next day we reached Alambagh without so much as a gun being fired at us. This was very strange for the mutineers might have annoyed us dreadfully, encumbered as we were with so many women and children (900 in all), besides our wounded, but I daresay they were glad to let us away quietly after the lesson they had got.

We halted at Alambagh one day and here Havelock, worn out with all his trying work, died.

Notes

1 European – there were mercenaries, Anglo-Indians and even, strange as it may seem, a few British soldiers fighting on the rebel side. Fairweather's references are interesting and this could be Drummer Jones of the Lucknow garrison who went over to the other side since his death is not recorded. It is interesting that he also refers to a similar incident at Delhi. For a discussion see an essay in Llewellyn-Jones pp 27–65.

2 Campbell – the man pledged to destroy the rebels and restore the British Raj, Colin Campbell had been born plain John Macliver, the son of a Glasgow carpenter in 1792. Throughout his life he retained a broad Scottish accent and peppery manner. He adopted the name Campbell as a *nom de guerre* and fought through the bloody Peninsular War. Gradually he rose in the service seeing action in the 1st Anglo-Chinese War and the 2nd Anglo-Sikh War where he had a bloody encounter with the Sikhs leading a division at Chilianwallah (though he got a knighthood). Then, in the Crimea, he became famous as commander of the Highland Brigade – his famous 'Thin Red Line' – at the Alma and other battles. Campbell was loved by his men, especially the Highlanders, with whom he had a real affinity, but as he had served on the North-West Frontier in the early 1850s he got on swimmingly with Indian troops too. He refused to waste men's lives unnecessarily and his progress towards Lucknow was criticised for its slowness. Many called him 'Sir Crawling Camel'. None of these criticisms seemed to bother Campbell much. Fairweather's stories of Campbell sleeping close to his men or being near the thick of action were typical of him. In countless actions he seemed oblivious to fear. For his services he was raised to the peerage as Lord Clyde. He died not long after the last of the rebels had surrendered, in 1863. Further Reading: Shadwell, *The Life Of Colin Campbell, Lord Clyde*, 2 vols, Edinburgh 1881 is the full and standard account; for an acid drop of criticism of Clyde as a general see, vol i pp 285–286 in the autobiography of his namesake, Sir George Campbell.

3 Pandi – also pandey or pandie – the term by which many British
called the mutineers was taken from the name of Mangal Pandey,
an agitated sepoy of the 34th B.N.I. who, on 29 March 1857, urged
his comrades on the parade ground at Barrackpore to rise in revolt.
When British officers tried to arrest him he drew his sword on
them and then tried to kill himself. He was unsuccessful; tried by
court-martial he was hanged a few days later. This martyrdom turned
him into something of a hero to the mutineers. Modern research
suggests the incident and the man were not quite so special. Further
Reading: Mukherjee, *Mangal Pandey*, New Delhi 2005.

4 Captain William Peel, who had already fought bravely in the
Crimean War and won there the Victoria Cross. He had with
him in India a Naval Brigade made up of sailors from H.M.S.
Shannon. There were three Naval Brigades during the Mutiny
(that of HMS *Pearl* also did sterling work and the third was the
little known H.M.S. *Pelorus* on the Irrawaddy River), and Peel
himself was to be killed in action during the final taking of
Lucknow. Further Reading: Rowbotham, *The Naval Brigades In
The Indian Mutiny 1857–58*, London 1947 is the definitive study of
their correspondence; for an in-depth look at Peel and the crew of
H.M.S. *Shannon* read Verney, *The Devil's Wind*, London 1956.

5 Leith-Hay – on 1st June 1857 the 93rd Highlanders had set sail
for India under the command of Lt-Colonel A. S. Leith Hay. The
regiment consisted of 34 officers, 40 NCOs, 10 drummers and
pipers and 650 rank and file.

6 Sebastopol – the seaport and crowning battle of the Crimean War
1854–56.

7 Subedar (or Subardar)-Major – the senior Indian officer of an
infantry regiment and adviser to the Commanding Officer on all
native matters.

8 Singh – he was also mentioned in the Commander-in-Chief's
Despatches dated 18 November 1857, for his 'daring' manner.

9 Khan – this was the first of two occasions when this native officer
won the Order of Merit for his bravery in the Mutiny (the other
was at the action recorded by Fairweather at Ruiya in 1858).
Indian soldiers were not only proud to win this honour but it
also carried an increase in pay. At the end of the Mutiny he left
the service, but when Colonel Wilde went to Umbeyla in 1863
Muckurab (Mukkurab) Khan turned up and insisted on serving
him as his orderly.

10 Lumsden – this was John Tower Lumsden, cousin of the famous
     Harry Lumsden of the Guides. 'He was a fine fellow – an
     Aberdeenshire man; and as he dashed forward, he waved his sword
     high over his head, cheering on the Highlanders, and calling out
     to them to fight for the honour of Scotland. As we turned the
     corner, a large body of the enemy appeared in sight. They did not
     apparently like the look of us, for they instantly bolted through
     a passage to our right, which led into a sort of inner court. In
     a moment we were at them; but poor Lumsden was killed, and
     Cooper got a cut across the head.' (Ewart, *The Story Of A Soldier's
     Life,* vol ii p 78, London 1881).

11 For a detailed discussion on the taking of the Secundra Bagh
     (Sikanderbagh) the reader is directed to the Introduction. It was,
     as Fairweather describes it, a hot and vicious fight with no quarter
     given and none asked. He is one of the few witnesses of the time to
     refer to atrocities committed by the British and his honesty makes
     his account all the more important. He does not excuse and he also
     does not condemn. One of the most horrible aspects of the Rising
     was that both sides displayed facets of what today we call 'total
     war'; women fought among the mutineers and got killed, while the
     British hanged and shot whole villages of men on a whim.

12 Rezai – a counterpane.

13 Clark – born in 1830, William Falconer Clark had been educated
     at King's College, London, and became an Assistant Surgeon on
     4 June 1854; he served in the Miranzai Expedition 1854, Bozdar
     expedition 1857, the siege and capture of Delhi, actions at
     Najafgarh, Bulandshahr and Agra, the 2nd relief of Lucknow, action
     at Cawnpore and capture of Lucknow 1857–58. He resigned his
     commission in 1864 and died at Dorking in 1906.

14 Smith – his official date of transfer was 12 December 1857; the 48th
     B.N.I. had mutinied at Lucknow on 30th May and, while most
     of the men went off to join Nana Sahib's forces, a small remnant
     stayed on and were loyal.

15 O'Dowda – he left the 4th P.I. after being wounded in the final
     assault of Lucknow and died at Fattehgarh on 21 January 1859.

16 Kajowars – native saddles.

6

Battle at Cawnpore – Fathegarh – Final Battle at Lucknow

A force was left at Alumbagh under Outram to hold the city in check until an army should return for its capture. The rest of the troops were pushed forward to Cawnpore in two marches at which we grumbled awfully as we did not know the occasion for such a hurry, and with so much baggage etc., etc. it took us double the time to accomplish which it would have done under ordinary circumstances. The first of the marches was the most wearisome I ever remember, for we only crawled along a few paces at a time and then halted and crawled on again. I still remember the appearance of the big breaching guns with their long teams of bullocks. The leading animals would make a start of a few paces and stop, while the others in rear did the same, until at last the movement reached the gun, which would move forward a step or two and halt. In this way, like a gigantic worm, did it wriggle along the road. We did not reach our camping ground till midnight. Here all we had to eat was a piece of cold salt beef with *Huntley and Palmers* sweet biscuits.

After we had gone part of the march there was a faint dull thud like a heavy weight falling on the ground. This grew more distinct. We became aware that some heavy fighting was going on somewhere in the neighbourhood. Before night it was evident that sounds proceeded from the direction of Cawnpore. We then heard that the Gwalior Contingent,[1] which had had been hanging like a thunder cloud on our rear had, during our absence in Lucknow, fallen upon the garrison at Cawnpore and driven it into the entrenchments there. The bridge across the Ganges was also in danger of being destroyed by the rebels. This would have meant Sir Colin's army would have been bottled up in Oudh and explained the cause of our forced marches from Lucknow.

As darkness came on we could not only hear the cannonade distinctly proceeding from Cawnpore but also the flames and smoke of that city, which had been set on fire in many places. The following morning Sir Colin, with a small escort, rode on ahead to Cawnpore while the rest of the army followed as fast as it could. Nearing the place we could see an occasional round shot from the enemy falling uncomfortably near the bridge of boats but we got over without mishap. There was much pottering of musketry going on between the enemy and our soldiers in their entrenchments. The latter seemed to be in much panic, popping up their heads, firing off their rifles, then popping down to shelter again. Although we marched past in front of their entrenchments we had not a man hit by a bullet from the enemy and so did not see the reason for such a panic.

We were encamped on the south side of the canal while the enemy held the city and suburbs on its north side. This was on November 29th. It appears that no fewer than 16 letters had been sent on to Lucknow to inform us of the approach of the Gwalior Contingent, but not one of them reached us as a body of Oudh rebels with two guns had been lurking near the road and stopped them all. It was only on the day we were halting at Alumbagh that a man at last succeeded in reaching us.

We remained here apparently inactive till December 6th, during which time all the women and children were sent down to Allahabad, while some reinforcements were received from below. Our camp at Cawnpore was pitched, as we thought, unnecessarily near the enemy for we were more or less always under their fire. One day a number of men were wounded in their tents and one shell knocked over three of the Highlanders. On another day, when the firing was more than unusually heavy, the 93rd Highlanders were paraded under shelter of a long barrack, but Colonel Ewart,[2] in a fit of impatience, stepped out from beyond the shelter of the barrack and had his arm immediately carried off by a round shot.

We all got heartily sick of this work for there appeared to be no end to it. We were all rejoicing at the thought of getting some rest at Cawnpore for the last fortnight we had been marching or fighting during the day and sleeping out at night with little covering (no tents or baggage being allowed), and often scarcely a morsel of food to be had.

On the morning of December 6th Sir Colin made arrangements to attack the enemy. The movements of the troops on the wide open plain at Cawnpore was the first time I had ever seen what I considered to be the real manoeuvrings of a battle. Our brigade, consisting of the 42nd and 93 Highlanders, were marched to the extreme left for the purpose of taking the enemy in flank and thus compelling them to evacuate the city. The Highlanders were formed in line and we were sent forward in skirmishing order in front of them, Sir Colin himself at our head directing our movements.

As we advanced over a sandy plain I could see the enemy's bullets knocking up little clouds of dust in the morning light like hail but the shot from the battery in front went over our heads being aimed at the dark line of the Highlanders behind us, which formed a better target than the dusty uniforms of our Regiment. As we got nearer to the battery, however, a shrapnel shell broke suddenly in front our line close to where I was. It knocked over seven of our men at once and, for a moment, I was not sure if I was hit also. While I was dressing the wounded men the Regiment was ordered to lie down on their faces while some artillery was brought up to pound the battery.

Our Regiment, then supported by the 53rd Foot, again advanced and a queer thing happened. A native sowar of some regiment suddenly rode up in front of our Regiment and straight at the battery with a drawn sword. We could see him actually charge into it, but with what results we never knew, or whether he was a madman, or one who had bolted over to the enemy. As we continued to advance the mutineers began to retire, while we pressed on, capturing several of their guns and driving them across the canal in great confusion. Had the cavalry and horse artillery been managed properly at this moment we should have killed an enormous number of them and have taken all their guns, but the man to whom the command was entrusted was sent by a circuitous route to cut them off from the bridge over the canal, bungled the manoeuvre and did not reach there until even we had passed the bridge. The enemy never made a stand after being once fairly set a-going, but retreated along the road to Kalpee as hard as ever they could, leaving the whole of their camp with enormous commissariat stores in our hands and dropping gun after gun as they hurried madly along. The infantry followed them ten miles while the cavalry and horse artillery pursued them five miles further. We then all retraced our steps to camp.

The trophies of the day were 11 guns (one or two large) and 7 mortars, while the amount of baggage of all descriptions was perfectly bewildering, the whole road as far as we went being strewn with wagons. Every soldier and camp follower was laden with plunder but no treasure fell into our hands. The loss on either side was almost ridiculous considering the results; only 54 killed and wounded on our side, while the enemy's loss could not have been very great for we saw few bodies lying about. I may mention that it was not very pleasant to see among the other articles strewing the road clothes and knapsacks etc., belonging to the 88th and other regiments. These had been taken by the mutineers the day before we returned to Cawnpore.

We did not reach camp till the middle of the night and so great was the confusion there that we were unable to find our place and tents. We spent a miserable night lying on the cold ground with no covering and nothing to eat; had it not been that I got a tot of rum from O'Dowda's flask and a cigar I should have been unable to sleep for sheer hunger. In the morning we found we were lying close to a bannia's[3] cart which was laden with ghee, atta etc., and we soon got one of our sepoys to make us some chapattis of atta and chopped up onions and ghee.

The Regiment at this time was commanded by Lieutenant Rynis[4] who had escaped from the mutineers (at some station in Central India), by the aid of a fine horse which he possessed and who was attached to our Regiment a short time before this; he was a cavalry officer, knew little about infantry drill, and his manoeuvering of us during the skirmishing, compared to that of the Highlanders, grieved the soul of Lieutenant O. Smith who had been the smart adjutant of the 48th Native Infantry.

We halted on that day after the fight to rest. Then the fighting brigade, as we were beginning to call ourselves, was sent off in pursuit of that portion of the enemy which had retreated by the Grand Trunk Road.[5] We marched all day and after halting at dusk to rest and refresh the men and cattle again resumed the pursuit. By daybreak we neared the place we expected to come up with them but were much disappointed when we heard from some villagers that they had all escaped across the Ganges. We held on, however, over the fields, down to the place on the river where they were said to have crossed. Here we had great difficulty in getting at them since the banks were treacherous quicksands in which we found several of the enemy guns stuck fast.

At last we succeeded in getting to within range and opened fire on the enemy's guns. Our practice was beautiful and after a short time they were silenced. Our Regiment was then sent on skirmishing over the intervening bare sand to capture the guns as it was observed that very few of the mutineers remained by them. We advanced cautiously at first until we got near when, as there were no shots sent at us, we made a rush upon them. Although we captured the guns there was no one to polish off. The enemy who remained by them had by now taken to the river. They afforded some sport to amateurs as they floated past; one poor fellow brought by the stream close to where I was standing tempted me to try my hand. I pointed my pistol at him, but said to myself, 'It is not my duty to kill unless in a professional manner,' and handed the pistol to a soldier who was standing by. He fired both barrels at the man but I was very glad to see neither of them took effect. Only one poor fellow remained among the guns, whom Ryves at once shot, as he was rabid against the mutineers after his recent narrow escape from them.

Thirteen guns were taken here not including the two found sticking in the quicksands. Many of the bullocks that had been dragging the guns were also stuck in the sands and the pulling of them and the guns out afforded work and amusement to the soldiers. One bullock that resisted all their efforts was at last shot and afterwards I saw many of them cutting steaks out of the animal to broil on the embers. Another bullock that engaged the attentions of the men for a very long time was eventually, with much difficulty, pulled on to solid ground, but was so little grateful that he at once charged his deliverers who scattered in all directions to the great amusement of those who saw it.

Thus was the end of the formidable Gwalior Contingent with its mighty 2nd class siege train. Very few of the men were killed but they no longer remained as an army, but were broken, dispersed and a rabble.

After that we marched back to Bittoor, the residence of the infamous Nana Sahib, where we remained for a day or two to raze it to the ground. I got a small piece of the carved woodwork of the Nana's bedstead which I sent home as a memento.

It was said that the Nana before fleeing from Bittoor had cast a lot of gold and silver vessels into a deep draw-well nearby and on top of them a lot of heavy planks of wood had been put in. We heard later that these planks were removed and a large quantity of gold and silver plate was recovered from the well.[6] While at Bittoor a large elephant died in the middle of the camp. Such a monster could not easily be dragged away or buried so coolies were made to cover him with earth and the grave thus formed a considerable hillock in the middle of the camp. This was the only dead elephant I ever saw and I never heard of one being killed in a battle, but I was told by a man who had been with Havelock in one of his engagements that a round shot had passed through the trunk of an elephant and the beast made the most awful uproar imaginable. I believe that a surgeon had to amputate the trunk and afterwards the poor beast had to be fed and watered by hand.

Shortly after this our Regiment was ordered to proceed along the Grand Trunk Road to guard the telegraph that was being erected. On Xmas Day 1857 we were encamped in a mango tope on the Grand Trunk Road and tried to make the occasion as jolly as possible by getting the band to play while we were at dinner and regaling the bandsmen with sweetmeats and a glass of rum each. Until we had been to Delhi I don't suppose any of the men had ever touched rum but, very absurdly I think, they there began giving it to them daily like Europeans, and though only the Sikhs took it at first, I found the Mahomedans now also indulging in the 'dream' as they call it 'sub rosa' laughing in their sleeve at the precepts of the Prophet.

Sir Colin reached our camp at Poorah on December 26th 1857 with a part of the army which remained behind at Cawnpore. On December 29th the force under Sir Colin reached the Khala Nuddee. A small force including my Regiment marched to attack a small fort at a place called Futteeabad which was found evacuated and blown up. But the bridge across the Khala Nuddee was found to be defended by the enemy. The 53rd Foot was sent forward to threaten the bridge while the guns plied on the battery defending it. When these were silenced the 53rd heard that Sir Colin was going to send his favourite 93rd to capture the bridge. The Irishmen would not stand that. Without the orders of their officers they rushed the bridge with a hurrah and settled the business. When the fight was over and all had returned to camp the Force was paraded and Sir Colin Campbell marched along the front of the line intending to say a few words to the 53rd for their acting without orders, but when he came in front of the regiment he was received with volleys of cheers which were renewed every time he attempted to speak. At last in despair, and not being very angry at the result of the fight, he waved his hand and retired laughing.

The army now advanced to Fatehghar which was entered without opposition but during our stay there several notorious rebels were seized and hanged. They were not particular about a gallows, but strung them up to a lamp post or the bough of a tree. On one occasion there, while I was watching an auction of some rebel's goods, I fancied that a man behind me was pressing rather rudely against me. I dug him with my elbow without looking round but he seemed to return the dig. I then turned rather angrily round towards the man and found that it was the body of a man that had been hanged on a tree close to where I was standing. The pressure against me was merely caused by the swing of the body when I jogged it with my elbow. It gave me a bit of a shock, but such scenes were so common at those times that the fact of a swinging corpse forming part of a crowd round an auction seemed to affect no one.

The refugees in the Fort here, after defending themselves for a considerable time, at last tried to escape down the Ganges in boats, but were nearly all captured by the Nana Sahib at Cawnpore and massacred with the other victims there. The Force rested for a considerable time at Fatehghar. During this time Major Wilde, who had been left behind at Delhi owing to his attack of cholera, rejoined the Regiment having come down with a force under General Seaton which had had several actions with the enemy en route; with him also Captain Cockburn-Hood[7] who had been posted as 2nd in command of the Regiment. It was well he came, for owing to the incessant change of officers, many of whom seemed to care little for the Regiment as long as they saw service, everything had been

allowed to get into confusion. No regimental accounts or books
were kept properly and up to date and the sepoys were allowed to
march about like a lot of coolies with ragged and torn uniforms,
one man wearing tattered trousers and another in a dhotie. When
they marched past my tent going on picquet duty they kept no formation, each carrying his rifle as he chose, in fact I was ashamed
of them, but the very day Major Wilde arrived in camp there was
a complete change. Indeed on one occasion an outlying picquet
had been left for 24 hours without any food. The men could only
appease their hunger by eating the cobs of Indian corn roasted on
embers and chewing some sugar cane for which some would-be
philanthropists condemned them for robbing the poor raiyats. Wilde
soon tackled the accounts, settling the Mess bills that had got into a
disordered state from the frequent change of Mess managers and the
deaths of officers, leaving unpaid Mess accounts, for no one got any
pay at that time and so were unable to pay their Mess bills.

On the night of January 26th 1858, when we were having a
rubber of whist after dinner, an order came for our Regiment to
march with a force under Brigadier-General Adrian Hope[8] against
a body of rebels estimated at 4, 000 infantry, 600 cavalry and 4 guns
at a place 18 miles off. The force consisted of 1 battery of artillery,
the 9th Lancers, Hodson's Horse, 53rd Foot, 93rd Highlanders and
4th Punjab Infantry. We marched all night and came up with the
enemy next morning posted in a ruined village called Shumshabad.
It had been a cold march through a thick frosty fog and the force
was halted to allow the men to get some hot coffee etc., before
advancing to the attack.

On our approach the enemy's guns opened upon us, but were
soon silenced by ours. Then my Regiment was sent forward at them
and captured 4 guns, tumbrels etc. As I followed the Regiment
through a narrow winding lane I suddenly came on a group of our
men round a tumbrel blocking the way and just as I appeared on of
them fired his rifle into it. A tremendous explosion followed and for
a moment I did not know whether I was in the air or where, but I

made a rush for the first glimpse of light through the smoke, and was only then able to find out what had happened to me. Fortunately, before we had commenced our march, seeing the night was cold and damp, I had exchanged my thin cotton uniform for a thick woollen coat and pants. This saved my life for although my clothes were scorched through they did not take fire and so only my face and hands suffered. Among the men who were near the tumbrel several were killed or died afterwards from their injuries.

While I was sitting after the explosion on the trunk of a tree a sepoy who had also been severely scorched sat down near me and began to examine his injuries. Getting hold of one of his fingers near the point he gave it a little twist when the nail jumped out of its socket. This seemed to alarm him and he said to himself, 'Ham nahin bachega'. Then, trying another finger, the same thing happened until he had tilted out several of his nails, exclaiming as each came, 'Oh ham kabhi nahin bachega', or "Oh, I'll never recover.' The scene became so ludicrous that notwithstanding my own suffering I could not help from laughing.

The place seemed so full of gunpowder that several other explosions took place and in one of these several of the 53rd were injured. The enemy's cavalry, which had been threatening our flank, were charged by the Lancers and Hodson's Horse. I heard afterwards that it was beautiful to see Hodson riding a little in front and in the centre of his troopers and to see how quietly he controlled their eagerness to press on by motioning them back, first on the right, then on the left, by a mere wave of his hand as he passed the hogspear (the weapon he always used), from one hand to the other while he rolled up his sleeves preparatory to the conflict. Whatever may be said of Hodson none can deny that he was a grand soldier and intelligence officer to whom the Delhi Field Force was mainly indebted for all the knowledge it got of the plans of the enemy.

It was several weeks before the burnt skin on my hands and face came off; when I appeared in public I was greeted with laughter as my new skin was pink while there was not a hair of any kind on my face. General Adrian Hope, who had known me for some time, said banteringly that all the ladies would fall in love with me if they had seen me then. But the pink colour soon became black in places from exposure to the sun, especially at the corner of the eyes, where crowsfeet formed from keeping my eyes nearly closed when marching in the heat of the day.

The 4th Brigade, still including the 4th Punjab Infantry, but in which the 42nd, Black Watch, had taken the place of the 53rd Foot, was now posted to the 2nd Division of the Army under Lord Clyde destined for the capture of Lucknow. This Division was commanded by Sir Edward Lugard[9] and our Brigade, as before, by the Honble Adrian Hope. The 4th P.I. marched from Futtehgarh on February 1st 1858, en route for Cawnpore where the Army was being collected, but the advance was not begun till March 2nd. But as the diary of the operations which I sent home is still to the fore, it is more interesting to repeat that than trust to memory:

March 2nd. Commenced advance on Lucknow. Took same road as last time, turning sharp to the right before we reached Alambagh, passing the deserted fort of Jellahabad. Little or no opposition – arrived at Dil Koosha, about 2 pm. Not able to go as far forward as last time, the enemy having thrown up a whole line of batteries from Hawks' House to the Martiniere. Round shot coming thickly in among us we were obliged to shift our camp behind an old wall. Our path was strewn with the bodies of some of the enemy whom Outram had cut up a day or two before. In the evening the Pandies having seized an old wall in our front and annoying the 34th Regiment very much from it, a company of our Regiment was sent out to support them but Hood, who commanded it, fancying he had been ordered to take the wall, went at it with about 50 men and cleared it in less than no time, although the enemy must have numbered 1,000. The Queen's Officer was rather disgusted at this, as he was the senior officer and ought to have commanded the attack. Moreover it was rather galling to see the small body, which had come merely as support, go in and take the place that had been annoying the 34th all the afternoon.

Five of our men were severely wounded in this affair, one of them having to lose his leg.

General Lugard, who commanded our Division (the 2nd) came into hospital next day and told the men he was highly pleased with the way they had behaved. Though our tents were pitched, we had to bivouac on the exposed ridge, with great grumblings from some of us old hands who have learned by this time that Pandy never ventures a night attack.

3rd. Our whole Brigade out on picquet. Nothing to do but loll under the trees and watch the enemy's round shot bowling over the open ground like cricket balls. We all the time safe behind walls.

4th. Remained on picquet till sunset then relieved by the other Brigade of our Division. Only one man wounded by a spent shot in the chin.

5th. In camp most of the day. The blackguards having as usual discovered the position of the Chief's Camp, have been sending long shot in that direction, some of them uncomfortably near us as our Mess tent is close to the Chief's tent. Engineers have been making a bridge across the Goomtee for Frank's[10] column to cross, which is expected today from Benares. In the evening when at dinner four new guns were opened on our flank from across the river and we thought we were in for it, as the balls were falling unpleasantly near, but after a round or two they unaccountably shut up.

6th. The Chief has shifted his quarters more to the rear. Outram with the 3rd Division and no end of guns crossed the Goomtee early, no doubt to take the enemy's batteries in flank; it is evident that the main attack is not to be from this side, as hardly a gun has yet been put in position here, only one or two of Peel's guns are on the ridge to the right of Dil Koosha to amuse the enemy, I daresay, more than anything else. They are working like bees we can see with the glass, throwing up earthworks and bastions all along the front. One gun gives us a lot of annoyance; they load it, run it round the corner of the Martiniere and fire, then dodge back before we can send a shot at them. It is really well served, and it is amusing to see how all our guns blaze away at it the moment the black nozzle is being pushed out; we have nearly knocked down the corner of the Martiniere but still the gun goes on unsilenced.

7th. A fight is going on somewhere over the river for the banging of the guns is incessant. No news from Outram, but I hope he is giving it to them tight. There is a slight difference in our numbers this time from what they were at the Relief; our Brigade alone being as strong as all the force put together. The home papers put it at 22,000 when it was only 2,800. I am recollecting that this is the anniversary of our fight at the Khan Bund against the Bozdars. Since then we have been upwards of a score of engagements and have marched upwards of 2,500 miles, in fact the sound of musketry has hardly ever been out of my ears since this day last year, how much longer is it to go on I wonder?

The cannonading is already beginning to flag and die away in the distance so, no doubt, Pandy is scuttling as usual.

8th. On picquet last night. Pandies very quiet but bothered by pariah dogs and jackals sniffing round me to ascertain if I was a dead body. People say what they like about old Mother Earth being the most refreshing of beds but commend me to a softer and a warmer one.

Not much firing on this side today. Pandy evidently begins to smell a rat and to doubt our demonstrations here.

9th. Stormed the Martiniere and other defences today. All the morning the heavy guns had been pounding a breach in the ramparts, when about 12 o.c. the 42nd, 93rd and the 4th P.I. got the orders to assault. We expected to have considerable loss as we crossed open ground between the Dil Koosha and the enemy's works, for it was swept in all directions by their batteries, but whether our fire had driven them out or it was not their policy to hold these works, I know not, but we dashed into them with little loss; the 42nd, who stormed some out-houses, meeting with the greatest number of casualties.

It was not the intention to go beyond this, but as it was observed that their next line of defence (a long loopholed wall with bastions for guns at short intervals and a deep ditch in front) was apparently badly manned, Wilde got orders to go and seize a village to the right not far from this wall, and on getting there and finding no shots coming from the wall he made a dash at it with some of the 42nd and succeeded in establishing himself inside, without opposition. Wilde then began moving along the wall, meeting with little opposition until he reached a bastion, where the fire from the neighbouring houses was so hot that he had to retire a short distance, leaving a gun which he had taken and spiked to fall again into the enemy's possession. As it was now getting dark Wilde thought it better to secure what he had already gained, and for this purpose, having sent back for support and getting 2 more companies of the 42nd, we established ourselves in a garden with four high walls, which we loop-holed and distributed our small force around. It was fortunate that we took up this position, for the enemy, thinking I suppose, we had retired, came along in force towards nightfall to re-man the works. We saw them as they came along towards us, apparently quite unconscious of our presence and chattering away among themselves. Wilde had got some of the Highlanders and our men behind the sandbags with which the gateway was blocked, and had given orders not to fire until he gave the word so, waiting until the enemy were within 15 yards, he poured in a volley on them. Completely taken by surprise they gave a yell and fired their muskets off, then sounding the advance and giving a cheer, they attempted to come on, but they had got a sickener and instead of coming on they made the best of their way back, carrying off their wounded but leaving two of the number on the ground dead, as we discovered next day.

About the middle of the night they made a second attempt to drive us out, but they could not get up the steam, so after a great waste of ammunition they shut up and allowed us to enjoy our nap again.

10th. Nothing done today except the clearing of the gardens in front by the 42nd and 93rd, while the whole line or wall fell into our hands. During the day we were all standing in the bastion from which we had to retire, and were listening impatiently to the sound of firing in front. Many of the stray bullets were coming into the bastion, open of course on that side, when Smith, with an exclamation of impatience, stepped out from the slight shelter we had and at once got a bullet through the back of his knee-joint. He spun round and I ran out and helped him back into the shelter, where I extracted the bullet. The incident afterward yielded some amusement to us for just before we advanced on Lucknow we had all been joking at Mess as to how each of us was to get the V.C., and the roll assigned to me was that Smith was to be wounded and that I was to rush out and carry him in from the field of fire. Although none of us got the V.C., it was agreed that I was the only one who ever approached the roll assigned him.

Our Adjutancy is an unlucky post, for of the 4 who have lately held it one has been killed, two have been wounded and one has died of fever.

The sailors' battery of 68–pounders etc., commenced towards evening to breach the second line of defence, which is the Begum's Palace, strongly fortified by earthworks.

We watched at night the shelling of the city in the direction of the Kaiser Bagh, both from our side and by Outram from the Secundra Bagh side. They seem, by the by, to have had quite enough of the Secundra Bagh last time, so Outram found it unoccupied this morning.

11th. Our fellows were grumbling at being kept in the rear, but before noon, much to their delight, we were ordered to join our

Brigade, which was to storm the Begum's Palace, a practicable breach having been made in it. We expected this to be easy work as the most crushing fire from our heavy guns and mortars had been kept constantly on it for the last 24 hours, and their fire almost completely silenced. But we were greatly mistaken for they here made the best stand they have yet done. The assaulting force consisted of the 42nd, 93rd, and ourselves with the 90th and a Regt. of Nepaulese troops in Reserve.

While we were waiting for the assault among some mined houses, a cannon ball from the Begum Palace rather startled us by coming through the mud wall (behind which I was standing for shelter) so close that I was covered with dust and debris. About 3 pm the head of the column issued from the garden where we were concealed, and with a cheer rushed across the open space to the breach, but here they came to a sudden stop for there was an enormous deep ditch which they had not observed, and over which they had no means of getting till some planks of wood were brought up. During this time the enemy kept up a heavy fire from the loopholed walls and caused considerable loss. At last, however, they managed to scramble in one way or another and got into the first court where they bayoneted about a hundred. But here another difficulty was met, for the gateway into the interior had been built up and no opening left but a small hole through which they could only creep on their knees one at a time. This of course took a long time, and a constant fire of musketry was kept on them from all the walls around. By means of pick-axes a larger opening was made and at last they got in in considerable numbers. It was not, however, till dark that the place was completely in our hands. Our loss was pretty heavy, but I have not heard what it has been all together. The loss of our regiment was 31 killed and wounded, including one officer named Stewart recently joined us, who was wounded in the ankle.

The 93rd lost 2 officers killed and some 50 soldiers killed and wounded.

There were about 600 bodies of the enemy lying strewn about the houses and gardens. It is really a wonder how we managed to take it at all considering the strength of the place, for our guns had positively done little damage to it, and I should think our Chief would be careful how he sends his troops against a place until he has some idea of its defences. It must have been a fine place when our fellows first got in, but they soon made a mess of it. Mirrors dashed to pieces, marble tables overturned and broken, the beautiful crystal chandeliers torn from the ceilings, smashed to pieces and trampled under foot, velvet couches torn up and every article of furniture broken to fragments in the eager hunt for valuables. It was a weird scene at night walking through the different courts of the palace, to see here a group of stalwart Highlanders begrimed all over, with piled arms, standing round a fire made of pieces of mahogany chairs and tables, etc., recounting the adventures of the day; there, a party of Sikhs and Goorkhas squatted on their hams round another, carefully revising their loot; further on in a dark corner you suddenly stumble over a heap of slain; in that raised building from which come peals of laughter and the sound of corks being drawn, a party of officers, to show their contempt I suppose for the tenets of the Prophet, had turned one of his holy temples into a taproom for the nonce. Passing through the various apartments you see the brawny legs of Highlanders reposing on silken couches – mayhap dreaming of home and auld lang syne.

We were not so lucky for we were obliged to make our beds on the hard pavement of another court from a corner of which came a strong stench of burning Pandies, bringing strongly to my mind the horrors of the Secundra Bagh. Wilde and I lay below the same blanket and I was glad to cuddle in beside his broad back for warmth. He had several times to get up and visit the sentries round. On returning from one of these visits he told me that a Highlander posted in a dark, lonely place near some rooms in which many hundreds of the enemy lay dead, was in a state of panic from having been fired at once or twice by what he was certain could not be a living man, as he could take his oath there was not a living man left in those rooms.

Wilde laughed at him, thinking it was only a Highlander's dread of ghosts that had made him imagine he had been shot at. But while he was trying to convince him that such a thing could not have happened another shot was fired from the death chamber. Then he realised that it was no imagination on the part of the Highlander and he soon relieved his mind by explaining that some of the men inside the rooms had probably been killed with an unexploded musket in their hands, and that as generally happens when a mass of men are shot down at close quarters, their clothes catch fire and that the muskets are exploded as the fire reaches them.

The sentry was satisfied, but Wilde believed that if he had not gone round the room the man would have deserted his post.

Wilde also told me that in following up some of the enemy along a street nearby he had been driven back, and that he had been obliged to leave behind one of his men who had been wounded, whom he had shut up in a bunniah's shop for safety, telling him he would come and rescue him the next day. In the morning, therefore, taking some of the men and a doolie with him he made a rush up the street, still held at the far end by the enemy, found the sepoy all safe in the shop and brought him back in the doolie.

An event of this kind does more to make men trust their Commanding Officer than anything else, for there is nothing so discouraging to men as they thought that they will be left behind when wounded, to be cut up by the enemy.

12th. Saw Russell,[11] the *Times* Correspondent, walking about taking notes. Our Brigade was relieved at night and returned to camp to get a little rest.

13th. Two thousand of the Nepaulese troops let loose upon the city to our left and they are going ahead well apparently from the sound of musketry and the smoke from burning houses. About

10 pm a tremendous musketry fire all along our position led us to expect an order to the front at any minute, but it turned out to be a false alarm.

14th. The Imambara assaulted and taken this morning but particulars not yet come to our camp. We hear that great numbers are now bolting from the city but that many are being cut up or taken prisoners by our cavalry.

After this, for about a week, the task of clearing the city was left very much to the Nepaulese troops who advanced slowly, burning and looting as they went. During this time also the Kaiser Bagh and other strong positions in the city fell into our hands without much opposition.

On the 21st, however, a column under General Lugard, consisting of a battery of artillery, the 93rd Highlanders and the 4th Punjab Infantry was sent to attack a Moulvie[12] in the heart of the city who had a body of the most resolute of the enemy with him and had fortified a mosque, the surrounding houses had been loopholed and the doors built up. Captain Cockburn-Hood with part of the Regiment advanced up a narrow street but suddenly came on two guns pointed down it and the enemy with the portfire ready. Hood told me he would have been there before they could have fired if he had only been followed by the men, but when they saw the guns they retired, leaving Hood alone. He pressed himself as flat against the side wall as possible when the guns were fired, and a grape shot caught him in the face carrying away all the cheek bone, making a ghastly wound. When brought to me it looked as if half his head had been carried away, as one flap of skin was hanging over the mouth and another turned up over the eye. Hood took it very bravely, poor fellow, and asked me to tell him at once if his wound was mortal? I was able to relieve him on this point but had to hold my tongue as to the probable effect on his appearance. He was a good looking fellow and it marred the look on that side of his face terribly, besides giving him great trouble for years by pieces of the small bones of the face coming away. He was naturally of an irritable temperament but the quiet way in which he bore his wound raised him much in my esteem.

While dressing Hood I heard that our C.O., Colonel Wilde, had been wounded in the groin while advancing with his men up another street, but that he had been carried back to the field hospital. I was disgusted with the result of this street affair causing so much loss without any success against the enemy. But the position was eventually taken by turning the enemy's left rear, our men getting into the mosque and killing a number there. The Regiment in this affair lost 17 killed and wounded, including Wilde and Hood, and the 93rd had 11 men wounded. When we returned to camp I ran over to the field hospital fearing that I would find Wilde mortally wounded, but I saw at once from his face before he spoke that it was not so. The bullet had been fired from a upper window and so had gone downwards. Had it been fired from the same level, that is horizontally, it would have penetrated the abdomen and been fatal.

Wilde, Hood and Smith being wounded, young Willoughby was for the second time left in command. After this the city was mostly evacuated by the enemy. One morning an orderly came and asked leave to go down into the city to get some loot. He said he had always been kept in the rear with me and had had no chance of getting any and now it was being plundered by the Nepaulese and others.

I said, 'All right, you may go out, but take your sword for there may be badmashes still lingering in the houses.'

In the evening I was lying in my tent on my camp bed resting when the door chink was raised and someone crawled through my bed in the dusk, pulled off his puggaree and threw it on the ground. I raised myself on my elbow and looked down on a man covered with blood, his arms and clothes hacked with swords. With difficulty I discovered it was my orderly. On asking him what it all meant he said he never could look up again. Had he been wounded in a battle he would have been proud, but to be wounded when looting was a thing he could never get over. He was disgraced and could never look his charibunds in the face again. After a time I got him to tell me what had happened. He had gone into a house supposing it to be empty, but on going into an upper room he heard some men making their way out of another door. He ran after them and gave the hindmost of them a slash with his word and then went back. While he was rummaging about, one of the men who had run away, not finding himself followed, returned and seeing only one man at once attacked him. The orderly's sword unfortunately broke off not far from the hilt and he thought his time was now come, but he rushed in and grappled the man. They fell and by God's grace he found himself uppermost and with the broken part of his word he cut his enemy's throat. By this time the others, who had bolted, also began to come back, but when this little blood-stained fury attacked them they fled and the orderly returned to camp, a crest-fallen man, bringing his enemy's sword with him. Having done up his wounds, some of them deep sword cuts on the shoulder and arm, I sent him away comparatively happy by telling him he had behaved like a plucky Sikh as he was and that no one could ever look down on him who heard his story. I also said that if his fight had taken place in a real battle he would probably have got the honour of Sirdar Bahadur.

Twenty-three years afterwards, in 1881, when I was Civil Surgeon of Lahore, I was walking through one of the streets when I met a genial native officer who came up smiling to me and said, 'Sahib, don't you remember me? I am your old orderly.' He then told me he was still with the old 4th and had risen to be Subedar-Major in it. He came to my house and we had a long talk about old days and I gave him my photo as a souvenir.

Notes

1 Contingent – this large army had been raised by the Maharajah Scindia of Gwalior as a result of an 1843 treaty with the British. Equipped, drilled and trained on the English model it had 2 cavalry regiments and 7 infantry battalions, 4 field batteries and a small siege train – 8,318 men. There has been some dispute over Scindia's

abilities to control his army. He certainly made some efforts but eventually they marched off to Cawnpore on 15 October 1857.

2 Ewart – born in 1821, the son of a Peninsular War veteran, John Alexander Ewart joined the army in 1838 and the 93rd Highlanders in 1846. He served with the regiment throughout the Crimean War and commanded the 6th company of the famous 'Thin Red Line' at the Battle of Balaklava. In the Mutiny his behaviour in the taking of the Sikanderbagh, where he got two sword cuts, led to an unsuccessful recommendation for the Victoria Cross. If he was feeling irritable, as Fairweather suggests, Lt-Col. Ewart does not say so in his memoirs: 'A cannon-shot suddenly struck me on the left elbow, completely carrying off the arm, which was merely hung by a thin piece of skin. I was aware that I had been struck violently on the left side, but did not know what had actually taken place, until I looked down and saw the bleeding stump. The ball had also broken the handle of my revolver and smashed my field-glass … The blow did not knock me down, nor did I feel any inclination to fall; but a soldier named Peter McKay … ran up at once, and tied his handkerchief tightly round the stump.' (Ewart, vol ii, pp 108–109). Recovering from his wounds Ewart went on to write his autobiography and command the 78th Ross-shire Buffs. He died in 1904 and is buried in the cemetery at Stirling Castle.

3 Bannia – a tradesman of some kind; in this case a grocer.

4 Rynis – an understandable misspelling by Fairweather; Lt W. C. *Ryves*, formerly of the 12th B.N.I. (the left wing had mutinied at Jhansi on 6 June, the right wing at Nowgong on 11 June), officially joined the 4th P.I. on 16 November 1857. He transferred two months later, on 29 January 1858, to command a regiment raised at Fatehgarh.

5 This well constructed highway ran from Calcutta to Peshawar with a spur running from Bombay and meeting the other artery at Aligarh. A shorter spur ran to Delhi. The road had been started in Mogul times but the British maintained it well. Stretches of the highway were formed of a strong limestone called conker that mixed with water and beaten down became as hard as cement. 'Every two miles along the Grand Trunk Road was a police station manned by three policemen. From 10 at night to 4 in the morning two out of the three policemen patrolled the road. In addition, horse patrols were stationed and checked every night by means of a verbal order which they were obliged to convey the entire length

of a district and then mail back to the originating magistrate to confirm the road was open and they were on the job.' (Raikes, *Notes On The Northwest Provinces*, London 1852 p 264).

6 'As soon as these heavy beams of wood were removed, a great quantity of silver plate – solid silver, be it understood – was brought to light, which owing to the action of the water, came up jet black. Among these silver articles, the State howdah of the ex-Peshwa, in solid silver, was fished up, besides quanties of gold plate and other valuables. Below the plate, which was merely deposited loose in the water, as if in a hurry, the sappers came upon an immense number of ammunition boxes tightly packed with native rupees and gold mohurs (each gold coin being worth 16 rupees at least), the value of the coin alone being currently reported in camp on December 27 to be over £200,000, in addition to the gold and silver plate and the ornamental jewellery.' (Gordon-Alexander pp 194–195). A great haul for the prize agents, one assumes, being worth (in 2011 values), more than £25 million!

7 Hood – he came from the 49th B.N.I., one of those regiments disarmed at Mian Mir on 13th May 1857. His official date of joining the 4th P.I. was 2 January 1858. Despite his injuries described by Fairweather, this officer rejoined the Corps in May 1862 with the rank of major and commanded the 4th P.I. for the next 11 years.

8 Hope – Lt-Col. the Honourable Adrian Hope was perhaps the most liked officer in Campbell's army; he was the youngest son of General Hope, 4th Earl of Hopetoun, an old warrior who had fought under Moore and Wellington in the Peninsular War. With an instinct for pleasing his men as well as being handsome, young and brave, Hope was destined, all thought, for great things as a general.

9 Lugard – rising from colonel to major-general during the 1857–58 campaign, Sir Edward was a solid soldier under Campbell but, in independent command, had the misfortune to be led a merry dance across Bihar in April 1858 by Kuer (Koer) Singh, the best guerrilla leader among the rebels.

10 Franks – a stickler for discipline, Brigadier-General Thomas Franks had formerly been colonel of the 10th Foot where he became notorious as a martinet. His reputation in the Army was that of a good soldier – he fought well in 1857–58 – but was a man who believed in the power of the lash. Half a century later Lord Wolseley would write of Franks in command of the

10th: 'No officer in the regiment would accept the position of adjutant, so harsh was he even to his officers. A lieutenant was at last found in another regiment who was willing to accept it, namely young Henry Havelock, the most daring of men in action and full of military ability. He often told me stories about this strange colonel he had then to serve with – a man as rigorous and uncompromising towards his officers as he was in all his dealings with the rank and file. Just before the battalion moved into action on the day of Sobraon, the colonel said to his men: 'I understand you mean to shoot me today, but I want you to do me a favour; don't kill me until the battle is well over.' It was quite true; they had meant to shoot him, but the coolness with which the request was made, the soldier-like spirit and indifference to death it denoted, the daring and contempt for danger he displayed throughout the battle, so won their admiration that they allowed him to live. But history tells us he never reformed.' (Wolseley, vol i pp 16–17).

11 Russell – the first and some might say the greatest of all British war correspondents; he was already a celebrity due to his reporting of the Crimean War and many officers now in India were old friends. Russell himself was well liked, 'a strongly-built man of middle stature, with a bright eye and a merry smile, speaking with a slight Irish accent', (Sherer, *Daily Life During The Indian Mutiny*, London 1898 p 152). What set Russell apart from other journalists were his intelligent and shrewd observations blended with wit. <u>Further Reading</u>: Atkins, *Life Of Sir William H. Russell*, 2 vols, London 1911 or, for a general approach, Wilkinson-Latham, *From Our Special Correspondent*, London 1979.

12 Fairweather is here referring to the Moolvie (Maulvi) Ahmadullah Shah, alias Sayyid Ahmad Ali Khan, a Madrassi of rich family who had even visited England and Europe before returning to India and being converted to jihad against the infidels. He was preaching revolt in Faizabad when arrested in February 1857 and thrown into gaol. Luckily for him he was released by the mutineers there on 8 June when they chose him as their leader. Despite, or because of, his fanaticism the Moolvie tried to instil some discipline and sense of authority into the Lucknow rebels but with limited results. He also proved himself an effective general in the actions at Chinhat and the siege of the Residency. His document, *Futteh Islam*, is 'a significant statement of the cause and nature of the struggle against the British.' (Taylor, *Companion*, p 215). The Moolvie escaped

from Lucknow, despite the attack on him and his fanatical ghazi followers, as mentioned by Fairweather; now calling himself 'King of Hindustan' and 'God's Deputy' he was a man with a 50,000 rupees price on his head. His end came when he was betrayed to the Rajah of Pawayan, who thought he could put the reward money to good use; the Moolvie was seized and his head sent in a sack to the magistrate at Shajahanpur. For a somewhat biased account of Ahmadullah's life and beliefs see Pandey, *Vision Of The Rebels During 1857*, New Delhi 2008.

7

With Walpole's Column – Battle of Ruiya – End of the Mutiny

When the Lucknow business was over we thought we would surely be relieved and sent back to the Punjab, seeing that Sir Colin had distinctly said he had only one more piece of business for the Regiment, and then they would get their leave to return. Moreover, we were again cleared out of superior officers and were commanded by a young subaltern while the men with the colours were reduced to 150. However, to our disgust, what remained of the Regiment was ordered to join a column under Brigadier-General Walpole[1] on a fresh campaign through Oudh and Rohilkund – and Captain Cafe[2] of the 56th Native Infantry was sent to command us.

I naturally did not wish to start on a fresh expedition with all my wounded and sick, so I went to Dr ----- our Principal Medical Officer,[3] to ask what was to be done with them. He said I must take them with me as there was no arrangement for a Native Field Hospital. I could not believe this after all the good service the Regiment had done for the Government, but Dr ----- said Lord Canning had refused to sanction a native hospital. So I was obliged to start on this fresh expedition with several country carts and my six doolies filled with sick and wounded – one of the latter an amputation of the thigh – and through a country devoid of roads. It was scandalous!

I bade Wilde, Hood and Smith a sorrowful goodbye and started with this remnant of the Regiment, the column consisting of the 42nd and 93rd Highlanders, the 4th Punjab Infantry, 9th Lancers and 2nd Punjab Cavalry with some horse artillery, in all about 4,000 men. We saw nothing of the enemy until one morning the column came to a halt as it was found that a Fort in our front called Rovia or Ruyaghari⁴ was occupied by them. General Walpole with his staff collected at the head of the column and seemed to be discussing the plan of attack. Our Regiment was in the front that day and I was so near I could almost hear what they were saying. I saw Brigadier-General Adrian Hope talking earnestly to Walpole, and I could see by their actions that Walpole disagreed with him, whereupon Hope left the conclave as if disgusted and came and lay down on his back near me. Shortly afterwards the column advanced, the Highlanders in front. On getting near the Fort we we were ordered to move down and support the 42nd Highlanders, who had taken up a position partly sheltered from the fire by the prickly pear trees which usually surrounded these forts.

On getting down there, however, Cafe found that all the shelter was occupied by the 42nd, so he moved to the left to see if he could find some shelter for the men. Not finding any, he suddenly charged across the open glacis into the ditch of the Fort, under the impression apparently that he that he would get some shelter there. In doing this poor Willoughby, who had been through so many hard fights with us, received a bullet just across the collar bone. He sat down on the glacis as Cafe passed and said he should go to hospital. Cafe did not find much shelter in the ditch and the men were being picked off from two bastions that flanked it. One of our havildars climbed a broken part of the wall and looked into the Fort. Seeing no one he called out to Cafe to come and they could take the place.

Only 50 men, however, were present as the other 100 were daily on rearguard, so Cafe sent back a note to Walpole saying he could go in and take the Fort if the general would send him reinforcements, but that he could not hold his position without help.

Walpole replied that if Cafe could not hold his position without reinforcements he must retire.

So Cafe gave the order and it was a case of 'Sauve que peut'; the men who were able scrambled out of the ditch and across the glacis into the prickly pear beyond, leaving 14 or 15 dead and wounded in the ditch.

In rushing back Cafe saw poor Willoughby's body lying on the glacis and he called to the men to bring it back with them but in the hurry to get out of the fire this was not done. Cafe therefore asked for volunteers to help him bring back the body. Two Highlanders and three of our own men immediately stepped forward and together they all went towards the body and dragged it back by its feet into cover. In doing this one of the 4th Punjab Infantry sepoys was killed and one of the Highlanders had his thigh bone broken; as he was lying on the ground he called out, 'You are surely not going to leave me here,' and Cafe again went out and helped the man in, but not before he had his left arm smashed above the elbow by a bullet. This poor Highlander, whose name was Spence, died of his wound, while the other got the V.C., as also did Cafe. The two natives got the Order of Merit.

Fifty years after this, when the occurrences were revived on the occasion of the Mutiny's Jubilee, His present Majesty caused a Victoria Cross to be given to the surviving relatives of Spence, along with four or five others who, if they had lived, would have received it.

In this disastrous affair the Regiment lost 11 killed and 36 wounded. Poor Willoughby had been on the sick list with a sore throat and was being carried along in a doolie when the column halted before attacking the Fort. Curiously enough, although as cool as anything in action, he was despondent when ill and that morning particularly so. When he heard there was the prospect of a fight he jumped out of his doolie in the highest spirits saying to me, 'This will be my – fight and your ----th'. So he went to fight in his slippers just as he had come out of his doolie. However, he remarked to me, 'I wish I could get a flesh wound for I feel almost sure that when I do get a wound it will be mortal.'

The finest Native Officer in the Regiment was also killed in this affair; his name was Subedar Hira Singh, a splendid specimen of a Sikh soldier and a great loss to the regiment.

I was kept busy with my wounded men and had tried to get some sheltered spot for them, but there was not a place out of fire from the fort, and the bullets came so thick around me as I was dressing that I expected every moment to be hit myself. Some of the men were again wounded after being dressed by me. My poor syce, who was holding my horse near me and who had been with me throughout the campaigns, was mortally wounded through both lungs. I was never so down on my luck and was thinking in despair what was to be done with all these wounded men when an orderly officer rode up and asked me what I was doing there, at the same time telling me the force had retired, and that we should be cut up by the enemy if we did not get the men out at once. I asked him how I was to remove all my wounded men with only two doolies as the rest of the hospital carriages were being occupied by wounded men from Lucknow. He said, 'Oh, I'll see if I can send you any carriages,' and digging his spurs into his horse he disappeared and I never saw more of him. By good luck, some of the men who had been on rearguard turned up; in searching through huts nearby they got a sufficient number of charpoys to carry those who could not walk, and so we reached camp which was pitched some 4 or 5 miles off.

When Muster was taken that evening all the men who were left in the ditch were put down as dead. But next morning one of them, who had managed to crawl into camp, told the ghastly story of how the enemy had poured out of the Fort with lanterns after the force had left to plunder the dead and to kill those still alive. He had feigned to be dead and when a man was trying to turn him over he suddenly grappled with him, wrenched his sword from him, and killed him. He then with much difficulty, as he was wounded in the thigh, managed to get out of the ditch and crawled painfully after the Regiment. This story had the worst effect on the men for it was a maxim of Wilde's never to leave a wounded man to be cut up by the enemy, even at the sacrifice of many lives.

And so ended this miserable affair, for the Fort was evacuated during the night and Sam Browne told me that when he made a reconnaissance next morning with his cavalry round the other side of the Fort he found there was a breach in the wall through which he could have taken his regiment three abreast. It was the most incompetent piece of business that can be imagined. There was no proper attack or investment of the place and the regiments were only ordered down near enough to the Fort for the men to be easily picked off from the walls.

One field gun went off at one corner of the Fort and, after a long time, it was followed by another from the other corner, and so this leisurely cannonading went on, while our men were falling fast and nothing was being done. In this wretched affair that fine fellow, the Honourable Adrian Hope, our Brigadier-General, was also killed. He was about the finest man in the Army, I should think, very tall and straight as an arrow with fair curly hair and the most genial expression of face. He was simply beloved by the Highlanders and they would have gone anywhere with him. When I heard he was killed I went to try if I could see the body as I had become so familiar to him through so many engagements. I asked a Highlander, who was walking up and down, whether he could tell me where the general's body was and he answered savagely, 'There he is,' pointing to a doolie. And there he was sure enough, as fine a specimen of manly beauty as could be seen, done to death by the mismanagement of an ingnorant nincompoop. The Highlanders would have shot Walpole I think if they had got the chance. It was strange that all three (Willoughby, Hira Singh and General Hope) were each killed by a bullet just above the collar bone at the root of the neck.

In addition to Cafe, Lieutenant Sperling[5] was also wounded, so that the Regiment was again stripped of its superior officers and left in command of Lieutenant Stewart,[6] with Lieutenants Stafford[7] and Hawkins[8] under him, all of whom had only recently been attached to the Regiment. On the second evening after this disastrous affair the funeral of General Hope and Lieutenant Willoughby took place. The graves were dug in a neighbouring tope of mango trees and the bodies were simply buried in their uniforms as they fell, wrapped in the cotton quilts off their beds. I did poor Willoughby's body up with own hands as I had previously done the bodies of Homfray, Oldfield and O'Dowda. All the Force was paraded and the bodies were placed on gun carriages and taken to the graves preceded by the bands playing the 'Dead March', alternating with the bagpipes wailing a lament. It was a sad and solemn ceremony for we had no victory to lessen our grief for the loss.

When we reached the tope the bodies were laid on the ground near their graves while the English Church service for the dead was recited in the gathering dusk, followed by a prayer by the Presbyterian minister of the 93rd Regiment. It was nearly dark before the ceremony was over and the three last volleys fired over the graves. My recollections are that there were three bodies, but I cannot remember who the third was for, of course, Hira Singh's was burnt according to the Sikh rites.

I think this Rooiya affair took the spirit out of our Regiment for the men felt they were just being expended and that few or any would live to return to the Punjab. I know the spirit was taken out of me, for I had seen the Regiment so often cleared out of its officers and their places filled with strangers, whose only desire was to drive the poor remnant of the Corps to new expeditions in order that they might reap honours and rewards, while most of them took no interest in the men; I was heartily sick of the thing.

The 4th Punjab Infantry was now reduced to 109 of all ranks. The Force continued to march but saw nothing of the enemy till we reached a place called Aligunge. Here we were joined by McQueen who had recovered from his wound, along with 20 men from sick leave, and he commanded at a small engagement that took place near here. The appearance which the poor old 4th made on this occasion was ludicrous; as usual, the bulk of the Regiment was on rear guard so that when the Force was drawn up in line previous to the advance the 4th P.I. was represented by about 12 ragged ruffians, 7 of whom were carrying tattered flags of one description or another which had been taken by the Regiment in the course of the campaign.

At Aligunge we were joined by Sir Colin bringing another brigade from Futtyghar and commenced our march towards Bareilly. We were glad to see more of the Chief and to feel that we would not again be led into such a wretched disaster as that at Rooiya.

We reached Bareilly on May 5th, 1858. The enemy had defended the bridge across the river with several guns but were hastily driven back with the loss of their guns. They then made a show of making a stand among the gardens and ruined bungalows of the cantonment, but our shells made it too hot for them. The 4th Punjab Infantry, which was covering some guns, was then ordered to advance and occupy some old barracks; this we did without seeing the enemy. McQueen thought it as well to advance a little farther and occupy a large tope of trees. This we did still without seeing any mutineers. He then divided the Regiment, taking a part with him to reconnoitre towards the top of another tope of trees to the left and sent a group under Stafford to occupy another position, while I was left with the remainder under Stewart.

In the meantime one of the men had climbed up a tree to see over some garden walls in front of us; after a time he called out that he saw the enemy collecting behind the wall. Since our men were all drawn up at the back of the tope, I suggested to Stewart that they should be made to line the front of it, so as to prevent the enemy getting into it and potting us from behind the trees, but he did not do so and soon afterwards down they came upon us, entering the tope and skirmishing in the trees. Our men gave a cheer and charged, driving them all helter skelter back to the garden. The men then, of their own accord, lined the outside of the wood, but were getting noisy and out of hand. Stewart had no control over them. He was a little dark man with a feeble voice and was still lame from a wound. The men seemed simply to ignore him. I tried to steady them, patted some of them on the back, said they had behaved splendidly, but told them to try and keep quiet and we should be able to meet as many as cared to come against us.

In the meantime more Pandies gathering in the garden. Soon they began to stream down upon us. Some were on horseback and some on foot. It was the bravest charge by the mutineers that I had seen in all our campaigning. This was the first occasion on which I gone into action without my sword and the only time I would have had any use for it. But I had a good double-barrelled pistol, a regular bone-crusher that Wilde had armed all his officers with. When one of the horsemen charging down our line stopped opposite where I was standing, apparently attracted by my white face, I quietly walked behind a tree, and steadying my pistol against the trunk, contented myself with covering him while my orderly, with a fixed bayonet, made an attack. The Pandy parried a fierce blow made at him and his sword broke off at the handle. My orderly then finished him with the bayonet. I took a silver ring with a red stone in it from his finger as a memento and still have it along with a bundle of papers sticking out of his pocket. I made these documents over to 'Thug' Wilson to whom was assigned the duty of trying rebels of this district. From him I afterwards heard that the papers contained the names of all who had attacked us; they were all ghazis who had been promised by a moulvee instant passage to Heaven if they were killed and instant passage to Hell for us if dead. I believe also that many were hanged by Wilson on the evidence of those papers.

Most of the attackers were shot down in front of our men, but as more and more seemed to be coming Stewart thought it advisable to retire to the old barracks which we had been originally sent to occupy. He gave no orders that I could hear and the men began to move off irregularly towards the barracks. On reaching these I met Stewart at the gate followed by a mob coming out again. He said we should be caught like rats in a trap there as there was no means of defence and no time to make loopholes in the walls. When the enemy saw us retiring they plucked up courage and came down upon on rear. The doolie bearers with their doolies and the ammunition mules then charged through the men in their front and the retreat became a stampede.

Fortunately at this stage a company of the 42nd, sent by the Chief to our assistance when he heard the firing, now arrived on the scene and moved in between us and the ghazis, who threw themselves furiously upon the Highlanders, many of them charging up to the very points of the bayonets, sword in hand, hacking madly in all directions. Many of the ghazis were so drugged with bhang that they did not know whether they were striking with the flat or the edge of their swords. Old Colonel Cameron[9] of the 42nd had a narrow escape; two of the ghazis managed to get round to the rear of the regiment, where he was on horseback and at once fell upon him. They were dragging him out of the saddle before they were observed. Fortunately, two Highlanders saw their Colonel's predicament and quickly despatched his assailants, but not before he had received several wounds. Everyone of the ghazis, of whom there were about 200, were shot down in front of the Highlanders.

A short time after it was all over I was moving over the ground when I saw a Highlander standing bareheaded above a huge looking ghazi hacking at him with a native tulwar he had picked up. I remonstrated with him for being so unmanly as to mutilate a dead body. 'Is he dead, begorr,' he said (for he was an Irishman), 'I have put four bullets in him and he's not dead yet.'. I could see the four holes about his heart and then noticed his chest was still heaving. 'Well,' I said, 'put a bullet through his head and put him out of pain.' The Highlander had a shield on his arm which the ghazi had been wearing. He said he had been carrying a green flag and was the leader of the ghazis. I asked him for the shield, but he was angry with me for having reproved him and refused to give it. However, before I had gone far away he sent the shield skimming through the air towards me with the words, 'There, you may have it if you like.' The shield is still in my possession and hangs in the hall of my house, where its appearance often leads to my having to repeat all about how it came into my hands.

After our flight, for it was nothing else, I had seen or heard nothing of the fate of the other two parties who gone off with McQueen. I afterwards heard that many of them behaved gallantly in cutting their way through the crowd of fanatics. A havildar, carrying one of the Colours of the Regiment, was attacked by several men and was wounded in the neck, but he killed two of them and brought his standard to safety. McQueen was described to me as stalking in the rear like an angry bear scarce deigning to retreat. It was said that he killed three or four men with his own hands. He was angry no doubt at having divided his small force and so allowed the mutineers to attack us in detail. Our loss in this affair, the last of many fights in the Mutiny, was 5 killed and 13 wounded. There was no more fighting at Bareilly and it is curious that our Regiment as usual came in for the worst of it. The city was evacuated next day by the rebels as they knew a force from Meerut was at hand to cut off their retreat.

The fighting strength of the 4th Punjab Infantry was now reduced to 100 of all ranks. Just eight months before, it had joined the army before Delhi 1,000 strong.

The 93rd Highlanders, with whom we had marched and fought shoulder to shoulder since their arrival at Cawnpore, played us out of camp with their band and bagpipes. Their colonel (Leith-Hay) made us officers tell the men how sorry his regiment was to part with them.

We had got a new Commanding Officer, Captain Stafford,[10] who formerly commanded the Hurrianah Light Infantry before it mutinied, the best officer of all those who had been attached to us, but unfortunately he joined us when all the fighting was over. We reached Moradabad in five marches from Bareilly without incident. Here we halted as the city contained a large population of Mahomedans. It was the time of the Buckra Red[11] and the Commissioner was afraid there might be a disturbance. He issued a notice that the 'Punjab Lambs' were approaching and that at the least sign of disturbance they would be let loose on the town; so effectual was this gentle hint that the Mahomedans did not dare to have their annual procession.

I may mention a curious incident that happened in camp here. A sepoy who had left his tent for some purpose in the early morning before it was quite light got attacked by some prowler for loot and had the points of two of his fingers cut off. On my visit to the hospital he came to have them dressed. This was done with lint which became saturated with blood. He left the hospital holding the wounded hand, grasped by the other at the wrist, with the fingers pointing upwards. He had only gone a few yards when a kite hovering above, thinking the stained lint a piece of meat, swooped down and carried off the whole of the dressing in his talons. I have seen kites carry off the meat from your very plate at a picnic but this was the greatest piece of kite impudence I ever heard of.

On reaching Meerut it seemed strange to be in a station once more where life was going on normally – ladies riding and driving on the Mall in the evening as if no war existed. It was a long, hot march to Rawal Pindi, to which nice station we were sent by the Chief by way of reward for our services. We took the marches easy and in order to get some sleep we generally struck tents at sunset and started for our next camp (from 12 to 14 miles), which we reached in four or five hours. The camels with our camp beds had preceded us and we at once turned in and went to sleep until the tents arrived and were pitched, when we were lifted into them on our charpoys and slept as we were able.

At Lahore the Hindustanis who had been left behind when we were en route to Delhi rejoined us. They had behaved well and had been employed putting down an insurrection in the Gogaira district.

At Jhelum I received a letter from the staff officer, Punjab Frontier Force, saying that in consequence of a paragraph in a

letter from Major Wilde to Brigadier-General Chamberlain bringing to notice the good service done by me during the period the
Regiment had been employed on service in Hindustan, which had
been forwarded to the Chief Commissioner, Sir John Lawrence;
the latter had requested Brigadier-General Chamberlain to offer
me the medical charge of the new Goorkha regiment in Hazara.
The paragraph referred to was as follows [Para 7 of letter No. 251
dated 15 April, 1858]:

> In conclusion, I beg to place on record in your office, the high
> opinion I entertain of the services performed during this cam-
> paign by Assistant Surgeon Fairweather. From the day the Corps
> left Lahore he has been unremitting in his exertions. On several
> occasions he has attended the wounded under heavy fire, and no
> man ever fell in action without receiving his immediate assistance.
> The natives of the Regiment have become much attached to him
> for his humanity and kindness.

Of course I was delighted, both that my service had received official recognition and that I had got a Regiment that was to be
always stationed at Abbotabad in a hill climate. But there's many
a slip 'tween cup and lip, and when the Gazette appeared, to my
astonishment, I found another man posted to the Goorkhas while
I was posted to one of the new regiments lately raised. I was sure
this must be a mistake. So was the Military Secretary to Sir John
Lawrence but, on reference being made, the reply was there had
been no mistake. The Military Secretary said that the only explanation he could give was that Sir John had been in the custom of
posting and transferring officers to regiments without reference
to the Viceroy while the Punjab was cut off from communication
with the Lower Provinces, but that when the country was opened,
Sir John had inquired whether he should go on posting as before,
or if they should be sent down for confirmation and the reply was
that the latter should be done.

My name was in the first list sent down for confirmation and the idea in the Punjab Government Office was that the Viceroy, merely to show Sir John that he was no longer supreme, simply changed one or two of his recommendations and that I, unfortunately, was one of the victims. Of course I declined the honour of being exchanged from my old Regiment with which I had been through so much into a newly raised one and was re-posted to the 4th Punjab Infantry again.

We reached Rawal Pindi on July 2nd, 1858 and were glad to be at the end of our weary march but we had not been there very long before the deadly monotony made us wish to go down country again. All the men who had seen much service were sent off to their homes on long leave and we all became cross and liverish from want of occupation and exercise.

And so ended my service with the 4th Punjab Infantry; I was transferred in May of the next year to the 4th Punjab Cavalry at the dreary desert station of Asnee on the borders of Sindh.

Notes

1 Walpole — considering the brickbats and criticisms thrown at him it is hard to understand why this officer gets an entry in the DNB while others, like Lugard, do not. Sir Robert had been born into the higher aristocracy and educated at Eton, receiving a commission in the Rifle Brigade in 1825, before a career that had seen no fighting whatsoever until the Mutiny. He remained in India until 1862 and by 1871 had become a lieutenant-general. He died in July 1876. In his history of the Mutiny the Victorian historian, Colonel George Malleson, singled out Walpole as the most inept commander. Discussing his campaign Malleson wrote: 'The expedition upon which he was now about to enter was not one likely to test the qualities of a commander. It offered no difficulties. A fort here or there might require to be taken, a disorganised band of rebels to be dispersed. To carry it to a successful issue, then, demanded no more than the exercise of vigilance, of energy, of daring — qualities the absence of which

from a man's character would stamp him as unfit to be a soldier. Walpole, unhappily, possessed none of these qualities. Of his personal courage no one ever doubted, but as a commander he was slow, hesitating and timid. With some men the power to command an army is innate. Others can never gain it. To this class belonged Walpole. He never was, he never could have been, a general more than in name. Not understanding war, and yet having to wage it, he carried it on in a blundering and hap-hazard manner, galling to the real soldiers who served under him, detrimental to the interests committed to his charge ....the course of this history will show that, though there ought to have been no difficulties, Walpole, by his blundering and obstinacy, created them, and, worse than all, he, by a most unnecessary – I might justly say by a wanton – display of those qualities, sacrificed the life of one of the noblest soldiers in the British army.' (Kaye & Malleson, vol iv, pp 352–353)

2 Cafe – William Martin Cafe was not a new officer; he had joined the army as an ensign in 1842 at the age of 16 and almost immediately seen action at the Battle of Maharajpore in the short Gwalior campaign, then fought in the 2nd Anglo-Sikh War. There was some dispute at the time about his VC award. He would rise to the rank of full general and died in 1906.

3 Since Fairweather declines to name this officer it is not certain but he is most likely referring to J. C. Browne, Superintending Surgeon and Principal Medical Officer of Campbell's army.

4 Ruyaghari – spelled a number of ways though the most common is Ruiya. Gordon-Alexander called it 'a miserable little mud fort ... the keep, so to speak, was enclosed by a high mud wall loopholed for musketry, with a broad and deep ditch on its northern and eastern faces, and approached by these sides through thick jungle. It had irregular bastions at the angles and one gate on the western and another on the southern face. The western and southern sides were, however, so weak as to be incapable of offering any defence being only covered by a large sheet of shallow water in front of the outer wall which was here so low that an active man could jump over it' (Gordon-Alexander p 290).

5 Sperling – his regiment, the 5th B.N.I. had mutinied at Umballa on 28 August 1857. After being wounded in the action described by Fairweather he later transferred to the 5th Bengal European Regiment.

6 Stewart – his previous regiment, the 64th B.N.I. had been stationed

at Peshawur where it showed strong signs of disaffection and was therefore quietly disarmed and later disbanded. He had been wounded at Lucknow on 11 March 1858, and later transferred from the 4th P.I. to the 6th P.I.

7 Stafford – P. C. Stafford had transferred from the Madras Rifle Corps on 13 February 1858; he seems to have left the service entirely on 9 May 1858.

8 Hawkins – F. R. Hawkins regiment, the 44th B.N.I., had been disarmed at Agra in May 1857; he transferred to the 4th P.I. in October and left the regiment on 21 May 1858 to become an Assistant Commissioner of Oudh.

9 Cameron – as this old officer lay down on the ground stunned, Colour-Sergeant William Gardner rushed to his aid. He quickly bayoneted two of the ghazis, as described by Fairweather, and attacked a third who was shot by another soldier. Gardner subsequently received the Victoria Cross, the last of eight men of the 42nd to win this supreme award during the Mutiny.

10 Stafford – W. J. Stafford was an officer who had already fought well in the Mutiny and Fairweather's praise was justified; in November 1857 he had formed the Hurrianah (Hariana) Field Force, composed of the 23rd Punjab Infantry, police and native levies to harass the mutineers in the Doab. He left the 4th P.I. on 28 January 1859 to take over the command of the 11th Punjab.

11 Buckra Red – I can find no direct translation of this phrase but there is an indication that 'buckra' is a Victorian slang term for superstition and it may also be a pejorative term for Muslims. So Fairweather is probably referring to a Muslim festival, or, less likely, Hindu.

Postscript

To those who have followed the history of the 4th Punjab Infantry thus far it may be of interest to know what followed.

The Mutiny made great changes in the Regiment. The paucity of officers had been made glaring by the losses in war and their numbers were increased. The new officers were in many cases married and, as the restrictions against ladies on the Frontier were either removed or in abeyance, more and more officers took to themselves wives. I would not venture to allege that this had any bad effects on the Force, but wherever ladies come in it is 'divide and rule' and so the old order changed. Instead of a rollicking lot of bachelors, free from domestic cares and ready to ride from one end of the North-West Frontier to another for a cricket match or a hawking party, men began to stick to their stations, to play croquet of an evening with their wives, to attend dances and picnics. Toy churches were built at the stations and a padre was appointed to visit them alternately. We became a civilised community and even started a hill sanatorium on Sheikh Bodeen, where the ladies could go for the hot weather and their husbands spend as much time with them as leave allowed.

This was the natural course of things and I only mention it to show how ways had changed since pre-Mutiny days. Although we old bachelors may have grumbled we were far from being unappreciative of the ladies in our midst. That the fighting qualities of the Force did not suffer was shown at Ambeyla and many other frontier engagements.

In order to understand how it was that the Punjab Irregular Force remained so loyal and behaved so well in the Mutiny it is necessary to enter a little into the general history. It was raised in 1849 after the annexation of the Punjab by order of Lord Dalhousie, and placed not under the Commander-in-Chief, like the rest of the Army, but under the Punjab Government which took its orders direct from the Governor-General. It was originally composed of 3 Horse Field Light Batteries, a garrison Company of Artillery, 5 regiments of cavalry and 6 regiments of infantry. It was officered in a very different manner from the line regiments – both cavalry and infantry having only a commandant, a second-in-command, an adjutant, a medical officer and sometimes a doing-duty officer who acted as a quartermaster.

All the officers were young, even the brigadier commanding, though a lieutenant-colonel by brevet, was only a captain in his regiment. With the exception of two majors and half a dozen captains none had higher rank than lieutenant. They were all selected men in the first instance, and remained select from the fact that only the keenest soldiers cared to stay long on the trans-Indus frontier where they had so few of the sweets of the service.

The duty of the Force was to guard the North-West Frontier from the raids of hill tribes (who were independent, owning no allegiance either to the Afghan or Indian Governments), from the borders of Peshawur in the north to those of Sindh in the south. Their motto was, 'Ready, Aye, Ready', and they were seldom long left idle.

Each regiment had an establishment of mules to carry ammunition, water and other necessaries in the hills, while for tents and heavy baggage any number of camels could be got in the district at short notice. Each regiment had also 8 doolies, with 6 bearers a piece to carry the sick and wounded, amounting to one per Company with a Sirdar Bearer and Mate to look after them. These bearers were recruited from a class called Kahars from Oudh and were marvels of endurance. Though poor in physique they never gave up even on the longest march and seemed to run along more easily with a heavy doolie pole on their shoulders than without it. They were plucky too in going under fire to bring out the wounded and some of them were killed doing so.

The infantry regiments were 800 strong divided into 8 companies, each with its complement of Native Officers. The men were recruited from all the fighting tribes of the Punjab as well as from Pathans and Baluchis of the neighbouring hills, who seemed to have little objection to fighting against their own clans. They were enlisted for general service as liable to be sent anywhere, even out of India. This was different from the old line regiments which were only liable to serve within Hindustan. Their uniform was khaki with puggris (or turbans) of the same colour, which were inconspicuous against the mud-coloured country of the border. When they were skirmishing on the barren, sun-baked frontier hills it was almost impossible at a distance to pick them out except by the flashes of the brass mountings on their accoutrements. In winter they wore poshteens, (sheepskin coats made in Cabul with the fleece inside), the outside skin was dyed a light brown and embroidered in yellow silk. The 1st Punjab Infantry alone wore rifle green and was visible at a distance.

The 1st and 4th Regiments of the Punjab Irregular Force were armed with the Brunswick two-grooved rifle (which was good up to 500 yards). It had a short sword bayonet. The other regiments had only the old Brown Bess musket, a very inefficient weapon against the long jezails of the hill men which could kill at 600 or 700 yards. Some of the Native Officers and men who preferred their own tulwars and shields for close fighting were allowed to carray them as well as regular arms.

The proportion of classes in each regiment differed according to the district in which it was raised. The 1st P.I., having been raised at Kohat, was principally composed of Afridis and other Pathans of the Kohat border. It was a splendid regiment and the men looked so well in their rifle-green, their puggris set high on their heads with a golden fringe hanging down on one side. My own regiment, the 4th, having been raised within the Five Rivers, contained a large proportion of Punjabi Mahomedans and Dogras from the Kangra and Kashmir Hills, besides Pathans, Baluchis and Multanis from the Dera Ghazi Khan district, and a few Hindustanis. There was also in it a larger number of the lately conquered Sikhs than in the other regiments. It was considered doubtful at first how these latter would behave and few were tentatively enlisted in some of the regiments. But the Sikhs are fine fellows; after being handsomely beaten by us they bore no ill will, but were ready to take service in our own regiments and have fought as well for us as against us. If I were to choose a man to stand by me in a tight place I would have a Sikh before any other native soldier whatever.

The regiments being composed of so many different races – generally on bad terms with each other – was a safeguard against a combination of evil among them; and their being stationed across the Indus prevented any chance of contamination from the Line regiments.

For my own Regiment, I must say the men looked a rough and ready lot compared with the regular Line regiments. Normal regiments were dressed in white drill and all alike in every respect. Our men presented many differences; the Sikh with his hair in a knot on the top of his head, the Pathan with a shaven crown but full beard, the Baluchi with thick black locks hanging round his neck and the Dogras and Hindustanis shaven and trim.

In the situation of the Punjab Irregular Force it was thought necessary to give Commanding Officers more latitude as to rewards and punishments then in the Line regiments. That this was only grudgingly given will be seen from the following incidents told me by Captain Wilde.[1] He was a great smoker and on one occasion handed his pipe to an orderly who refused to touch it because he was a Sikh. Wilde knew well that though Sikhs may not smoke they may touch tobacco. He therefore held a panchayet (or committee) of five Sikhs of the Regiment and asked if it was unlawful for one of them to touch tobacco. They at once said that so far from being unlawful it was likely that the orderly's father grew and sold tobacco. Probably this man had other things against him as well as Wilde turned him out of the Regiment. The Brigadier was averse to confirming the sentence and only did so when Wilde told him plainly that he could not remain in the Regiment otherwise.

After the Mutiny the Force was increased by amalgamation with the Corps of Guides, the 4 local Sikh Corps raised in 1846, and the Hazara Gurkha Battalion (now the 5th Gurkhas). It name was changed to the Punjab Frontier Force and it went on to garrison the whole of the North-West Frontier from Hazara down to Sindh, except the important station of Peshawur which was garrisoned by British troops.

From the initial letters of the Force (P.F.F.) the officers came to be known as Piffers. And that is how they are generally known now, the successors of 'the copper-bottomed men John Lawrence loved.'

Notes

1   Wilde – Alfred returned to India in 1859, now promoted to brevet Lt-Colonel and led the 4th P.I. in the expedition against the Mahsud Waziris. On 3rd March 1862 he was appointed Commandant of the Corps of Guides and commanded them in the Ambela (Umbeyla) expedition in 1863. In February 1865 he took over as Commandant of the Punjab Irregular Force with the rank of brigadier-general. Three years later he was given command in yet another expedition against the Black Mountain tribes and fanatics. He finally left India in 1871 and in 1877 became a member of the Council of India. He died on 7 February 1878 just prior to the start of the 2nd Afghan War. Fairweather was to outlive his old friend by almost 40 years.

Bibliography

Allen, C. *Soldier Sahibs: The Daring Adventurers Who Tamed India's Northwest Frontier* (London 2000)

Anon. *History of the 4th Regiment, Punjab Infantry* (Calcutta 1894)

Anon. *History of the 20th, Duke of Cambridge's Own) Infantry: Brownlow's Punjabis* (Devonport 1909)

Barter, R. *The Siege of Delhi: Mutiny Memoirs of an Old Officer* (London 1984)

Blomfield, D. (ed.) *Lahore to Lucknow: The Indian Mutiny Journal of Arthur Moffatt Lang* (London 1992)

Butler, Lt-Col. L. *The Annals of the King's Royal Rifle Corps Vol III* (London 1926)

Cantlie, Lt-Gen. Sir N. *A History of the Army Medical Department* Vol II (Edinburgh 1974)

Cave-Browne, Rev. J. *The Punjab and Delhi in 1857: Being A Narrative Of The Measures By Which The Punjab Was Saved And Delhi Recovered During The Indian Mutiny* 2 vols (Edinburgh 1861)

Collier, R. *The Sound of Fury: An Account of the Indian Mutiny* (London 1963)

Collister, P. *'Hellfire Jack!' VC: The Life and Times of General Sir William Olpherts VC, GCB 1822–1902* (London 1989)

Crawford, Lt–Col. D. *A History of the Indian Medical Service* 2 vols (London 1914)

_____ *Roll of the Indian Medical Service 1615–1930* (London 1930)

Creagh, Sir O. and Humphris, E. *The Victoria Cross 1856–1920: A Complete Record of the Recipients of the Victoria Cross from its Inception in 1856, to the 29th October 1920 With Descriptions of the Deeds and Services For Which the Award Was Given and With Many Biographical and Other Details* (Polstead 1985)

Dalrymple, W. *The Last Mughal: The Fall of a Dynasty, Delhi 1857* (London 2006)

Daly, Maj. H. *Memoirs of General Sir Henry Dermot Daly GCB, CIE, Sometime Commander Of Central India Horse, Political Assistant For Western Malwa, Etc., Etc* (London 1905)

David, S. *The Indian Mutiny 1857* (London 2002)

Dey, R. *A Brief Account of the Punjab Frontier Force from its Origination in 1849 to Redistribution on 31.3.1903* (Abbottobad 1903)

Ewart, Lt–Gen. J. *The Story of a Soldier's Life: Or Peace, War and Mutiny Vol II* (London 1881)

Fabb, J. *The Victorian and Edwardian Army from Old Photographs* (London 1975)

Fayrer, Surg–Gen. Sir J. *Recollections of My Life* (Edinburgh 1900)

Forbes-Mitchell, Sgt. W. *Reminiscences of the Great Mutiny 1857–59: Including the Relief, Siege and Capture Of Lucknow and the Campaigns In Rohilcund and Oude* (London 1893)

Gimlette, Lt–Col. G. *A Postscript to the Records of the Indian Mutiny: An Attempt to Trace the Subsequent Careers and Fate of the Rebel Bengal Regiments, 1857–1858* (London 1927)

Gordon-Alexander, Lt–Col. W. *Recollections of a Highland Subaltern During the Campaigns of the 93rd Highlanders in India Under Colin Campbell, Lord Clyde, In 1857, 1858 and 1859* (London 1898)

Hibbert, C. *The Great Mutiny: India 1857* (London 1978)

Holmes, R. *Sahib: The British Soldier in India 1750–1914* (London 2005)

Holmes, T. *A History of the Indian Mutiny: Fifth Revised Edition* (London 1904)

Home, Surg–Gen. Sir A. *Service Memories* (London 1912)

Jones, Capt O. *Recollections of a Winter Campaign in India in 1857–58* (London 1859)

Kaye, Sir J. & Malleson, Col. G. *History of the Indian Mutiny of 1857–8* 6vols (London 1889)

Lee-Warner, Sir W. *Memoirs of Field-Marshal Sir Henry Wylie Norman GCB, GCMG, CIE* (London 1908)

Llewellyn-Jones, R. *The Great Uprising in India 1857–58: Untold Stories Indian and British* (Woodbridge 2007)

Lumsden, Gen. Sir P.) & Elsmie, G. *Lumsden of the Guides: A Sketch of the Life of Lieut.-Gen. Sir Harry Burnett Lumsden KCSI CB with Sketches from his Correspondence and Occasional Papers* (London 1899)

Moreman, T. *The Army in India and the Development of Frontier Warfare 1849–1947* (London 1998)

Munro, Surg-Gen. *Records of Service and Campaigning in Many Lands Vol II* (London 1887)

Paget, Lt-Col. W. & Mason, Lt. A.H. *A Record of the Expeditions Against the North-West Fronteir Tribes Since The Annexation Of The Punjab* (London 1884)

Raynor, A. (ed.) *Mutiny Records: Correspondence & Reports* 4 vols (Lahore 1911)

Reeves, N. (ed.) *An Army Doctor in the Indian Revolt 1857–58: The Diary Of Assistant-Surgeon Henry Kelsall, H.M. 20th Regiment Of Foot* (Nedlands 1984)

Roberts, Lord F.M. *Forty-One Years in India: From Subaltern to Commander-In-Chief Vol I* (London 1897)

Russell, W. *My Diary in India: In the Year 1858–59* 2 vols (London 1860)

Sattin, A. (ed.) *An Englishwoman in India: The Memoirs of Harriet Tytler 1828–1858* (Oxford 1986)

Shand, A. *General John Jacob: Commandant Of The Sind Irregular Horse And Founder Of Jacobabad* (London 1900)

Spilsbury, J. *The Indian Mutiny* (London 2007)

Taqui, R. *Lucknow 1857: The Two Wars Of Lucknow: The Dusk of an Era* (Lucknow 2001)

Toomey, T. *Heroes of the Victoria Cross* (London 1895)

Taylor, A. *A Companion to theIndian Mutiny of 1857* (New Delhi 1996)

Vaughan, Gen. Sir J. *My Service in the Indian Army – and After* (London 1904)

Wise, J. *The Diary of a Medical Officer during the Great Indian Mutiny of 1857* (Cork 1894)

Wolseley, FM. *The Story of a Soldier's Life Vol I* (London 1903)

Yalland, Z. *Boxwallahs: The British In Cawnpore 1857–1901* (Norwich 1994)

Yule, Col. H. & Burnell, A. *Hobson-Jobson: A Glossary Of Colloqual Anglo-Indian Words And Phrases And Of Kindred Terms, Entymological, Historical, Geographical And Discursive* (London 1903)

Index

Afghanistan 25, 85, 97, 98, 118
Agra 7, 13, 37, 84, 95, 123, 125, 126, 127, 128, 129, 131, 133, 134,
   35, 155, 197
Alambagh / Alumbagh 14, 152, 153, 157, 158, 167

Bannu 25, 31, 34, 85, 87
Bareilly 13, 48, 189, 192
Bombay 22, 23, 40, 82, 86, 114, 131, 133, 136, 178
Bozdars 11, 27, 29, 30, 31, 77, 79, 88, 89, 116, 169
Browne, Gen. Sir Sam 31, 63, 64, 68, 83, 187
Brownlow, F.M. Sir Charles 99, 116, 117, 205

Cafe, Capt. William 47, 183, 184, 185, 188, 196
Calcutta 14, 21, 22, 32, 40, 52, 55, 58, 59, 80, 96, 178, 205
Cameron, Col. 191, 197
Campbell, Gen. Sir Colin 14, 15, 16, 38, 39, 40, 42, 45, 48, 52,
   120, 143, 144, 146, 152, 153, 163, 164, 179, 206

Cawnpore 7, 13, 14, 16, 18, 37, 38, 39, 45, 51, 52, 123, 129, 132, 135, 136, 150, 151, 155, 157, 158, 159, 160, 161, 163, 164, 165, 167, 169, 171, 173, 175, 177, 178, 179, 181, 207
Chamberlain, Brig-Gen. Neville 27, 28, 29, 31, 34, 77, 87, 194
Clark, Asst-Surg. William 123, 149, 155
Cockburn-Hood, Capt. 164, 175
Coke, Major John 25, 26, 29, 30, 76, 77, 78, 84, 86, 106, 109, 110

Dalhousie, Governor-General Lord 16, 23, 79, 87, 200
Delhi 7, 9, 13, 16, 18, 19, 31, 33, 34, 36, 48, 51, 58, 79, 82, 85, 87, 89, 91, 92, 95, 96, 99, 101, 103, 104, 105, 107, 108, 109, 111, 113, 114, 115, 117, 118, 119, 120, 121, 123, 124, 128, 132, 134, 136, 141, 153, 154, 155, 163, 164, 166, 178, 181, 192, 193, 205, 206, 207
Dera Ghazi Khan 22, 25, 26, 27, 29, 61, 62, 63, 66, 68, 71, 72, 77, 78, 109, 202
Dera Ismail Khan 25, 72, 73, 74, 90
Dhulleepghur, Fort 74, 85
Dilkusha / Dilkoosha, Palace 41, 143, 150, 151, 152

Earle, Lt. 63, 71, 78, 83, 85, 101
Ewart, Lt-Col. Sir John 20, 43, 44, 155, 159, 178, 206

Fateghar / Futteghar / Futtehgarh 167,
Fairweather, Deputy-Surgeon James 3, 10, 11, 12, 13, 14, 16, 17, 18, 19, 20, 21, and importance of Peshawar 25; 26, 27, and error over greased cartridges 31; 34, 35, 36, 37, 38, 39, 40, 41, 44, 45, 46, 47, 48, 50, 52, 79, 81, and Nicholson brothers 83; 84, 85, 86, 88, and McQueen 96; 97, 98, 107, 119, 120, 121, 132, 133, 136, 153, and Khan 154; and account of British atrocities 155; 178, and Hood 179; and Ahmadullah Shah 180; 181, 194, 196, 197, 203
Franks, Brig-Gen. Thomas 14, 179

Goorkha 34, 106, 118, 173, 194
Gordon-Alexander, Lt. William 20, 39, 43, 44, 47, 52, 53, 179, 196, 206
Grant, Col. J. Hope 129, 130, 134
Greathed, Col. Edward 16, 37, 38, 116, 123, 126, 129, 132
Gwalior Contingent 13, 45, 87, 135, 158, 162, 177, 196

Havelock, Maj-Gen. Sir Henry 14, 88, 125, 129, 131, 134, 135, 137, 139, 143, 153, 163, 180
Hawkins, Lt. F. 188, 197
Hodson, Lt. William 12, 47, 84, 109, 118, 119, 165, 166
Homfray, Lt. R. 36, 78, 88, 89, 95, 99, 103, 105, 112, 116, 120, 121, 188
Hope, Brig-Gen. Adrian 46, 47, 49, 165, 167, 179, 184, 187, 188
Hospitals 17, 18, 95
Hughes, Gen. William 66, 74, 77, 84

Jackson, Surgeon 59, 60, 61, 62
Jacob, Brig-Gen. John 76, 86, 87, 207
Jones, Lt-Col. John 114, 121

Kaiser Bagh 149, 152, 171, 175
Kelsall, Surgeon Henry 14, 20, 207
Khan, Subedar Mukarrab / Muckurab / Mukkurab 44, 147, 154
Kirk, Dr. I. 55, 57, 58, 59, 79, 92

Lahore 13, 23, 25, 34, 59, 61, 83, 89, 91, 99, 102, 103, 104, 111, 112, 117, 177, 193, 194, 205, 207
Lane, Lt. C. 124, 131, 132
Lang, Lt. Arthur 38, 39, 44, 45, 133
Lawrence, Sir Henry 19, 22, 23, 24, 84, 117, 118
Lawrence, Sir John 27, 33, 34, 68, 69, 84, 86, 104, 116, 117, 120, 194, 203
Leith-Hay, Lt-Col. A. 146, 154, 192

Lucknow 7, 11, 13, 14, 16, 18, 19, 20, 24, 38, 39, 40, 42, 45, 46, 47, 51, 84, 96, 120, 121, 124, 129, 131, 133, 135, 137, 139, 141, 143, 145, 147, 149, 150, 151, 153, 154, 155, 157, 158, 167, 171, 180, 181, 183, 186, 197, 205, 206, 207
Lugard, Brig-Gen. Edward 167, 168, 175, 179, 195
Lumsden, Lt. Billy 106, 118
Lumsden, Gen. Harry 22, 23, 52, 118, 155, 207
Lumsden, Capt. John 43, 147, 155

Malagarh, Fort 124, 132
Mansfield, Maj-Gen. Sir William 45
Maxwell, Surgeon Thomas 63, 84
McQueen, Lt. John 13, 35, 36, 40, 42, 44, 93, 96, 97, 104, 114, 115, 119, 121, 126, 127, 129, 140, 147, 148, 149, 188, 189, 192
Mecham, Capt. R. 30, 77, 78, 87, 88
Medley, Capt. Julius 27, 63, 68, 84, 109
Meerut 16, 33, 89, 119, 120, 192, 193
Mian Mir 22, 58, 59, 60, 132, 179
Mooltan 61, 62, 70, 81, 82
Moolvie Ahmadullah Shah 180, 181
Munro, Surgeon William 14, 48, 53, 207
Murdan 94, 95
Mynpoorie 139, 134, 145

Nana Sahib 38, 129, 135, 136, 155, 162, 164
Narinji 35, 94, 95, 104
Naval Brigade 20, 42, 142, 143, 154
Nicholson, Lt. Charles 63, 65, 83, 111, 119
Nicholson, Brig-Gen. John 33, 35, 65, 75, 83, 85, 104, 105, 109, 111, 112, 118, 119, 120

O'Dowda, Lt. 151, 155, 161, 188
Oldfield, Lt. F. 129, 134, 145, 148, 149, 150, 151, 188
Osborn, Lt. R. 124, 126, 132

Oudh 40, 42, 46, 137, 140, 143, 158, 183, 197, 201

Paget, Capt. William 27, 52, 76, 86, 88, 207
Paul, Capt. 36, 38, 42, 44, 45, 63, 65, 71, 74, 83, 93, 104, 127, 144, 146, 149, 150, 151
Peel, Capt. William 20, 42, 43, 146, 154, 168
Peshawar 25, 34, 178, 200, 203
Probyn, Gen. Sir Dighton 63, 84, 128, 133
Punjab Irregular Force 7, 10, 22, 23, 28, 55, 61, 87, 117, 118, 133, 200, 201, 202, 203

Ranigunge 58
Rawal Pindi 34, 36, 50, 104, 105, 195
Regiments:
(Queen's Army)
  8th Hussars 21
9th Lancers 17, 37, 59, 81, 109, 111, 128, 129, 130, 134, 141, 165, 184
42nd Highlanders 46, 47, 18, 184
53rd Foot 40, 41, 141, 160, 163, 165, 167
60th Rifles 36, 107, 109, 121
93rd Highlanders 14, 20, 39, 40, 41, 44, 47, 48, 50, 137, 143, 145, 148, 154, 159, 165, 175, 178, 184, 192, 206
Royal Atillery 42, 131
(H.E.I.C. Army)
Corps of Guides 23, 26, 79, 118, 203
  1st Punjab Cavalry 66, 74, 86, 133
  2nd Punjab Cavalry 27, 31, 63, 64, 184
  3rd Punjab Cavalry 27, 76
  4th Punjab Cavalry 13, 27, 195
  1st Punjab Infantry 25, 29, 76, 77, 89, 106, 201
  2nd Punjab Infantry 29, 30, 98, 123, 141, 154
  4th Punjab Infantry 10, 13, 14, 22, 27, 29, 30, 38, 39, 40, 41, 42, 43, 46, 48, 50, 51, 83, 93, 96, 110, 117, 124, 125, 126, 129, 143,

151, 152, 165, 167, 175, 184, 185, 188, 189, 192, 195, 199
  5th Punjab Infantry 67, 95
Roberts, Lt. Frederick 43, 44, 53, 68, 85, 95, 97, 98, 120, 207
Rotton, Rev. John 18, 51, 114, 120, 121
Ruiya / Rooiya 8, 47, 48, 49, 154, 183, 188, 189, 196
Russell, William Joward 17, 18, 20, 40, 41, 51, 52, 80, 81, 174, 180,
  207
Ryves, Lt. W. / Rynis 161, 162, 178

Sikanderbagh / Secundra Bagh / Secandra Bagh 7, 15, 42, 43,
  155, 178
Singh, Subedar-Major Gokul / Gokal 41, 44, 146, 154
Singh, Subedar Hira 40, 186, 187, 188
Singh, Sepoy Nirpat 46, 47
Smith, Lt. O. 58, 109, 111, 120, 151, 155, 161, 171, 176, 184
Sperling, Lt. 188, 196
Stafford, Lt. W. 188, 189, 192, 197
Stewart, Lt. 172, 188, 189, 190, 191, 197
Stewart, Dr. Lindsay 55, 57, 79, 105, 109, 115, 116

Tytler, Harriet 9, 51, 120, 207

Vancouver 9, 51
Vaughan, Maj. J. Luther 35, 66, 67, 95, 96, 98, 207
Victoria Cross 14, 83, 84, 96, 118, 119, 133, 154, 178, 185, 197,
  206, 207

Walpole, Brig-Gen. Robert 8, 47, 48, 183, 184, 185, 187, 189,
  191, 193, 195, 196, 197
Watson, Gen. Sir John 128, 133, 134
Wilde, Lt-Gen. Alfred 5, 13, 29, 30, 36, 50, 63, 65, 66, 68, 70, 71,
  73, 74, 75, 82, 83, 92, 93, 94, 95, 96, 99, 102, 103, 104, 105, 109,
  110, 112, 123, 124, 154, 164, 165, 170, 173, 174, 176, 184, 187,
  190, 194, 202, 203

Willoughby, Lt. Edward 42, 44, 47, 131, 136, 146, 149, 176, 184, 185, 187, 188
Windham, Maj-Gen. Sir Charles 45, 51
Wilson, Lt-Gen. Sir Archdale 112, 113, 115, 119, 120, 190

Yusafzai 7, 11, 13, 27, 35, 67, 89, 93, 97, 98, 118
Younghusband, Lt. George 89, 95, 96, 128, 133